PROFIT FROM
HAPPINESS

D0814747

Profit from
HAPPINESS

---- * ----

The Unity of Wealth, Work, and Personal Fulfillment

JAKE DUCEY

A TarcherPerigee Book

tarcherperigee

An imprint of Penguin Random House LLC
375 Hudson Street
New York, New York 10014

Copyright © 2016 by Jake Ducey
Penguin supports copyright. Copyright fuels creativity, encourages diverse
voices, promotes free speech, and creates a vibrant culture. Thank you
for buying an authorized edition of this book and for complying with
copyright laws by not reproducing, scanning, or distributing any part
of it in any form without permission. You are supporting writers and
allowing Penguin to continue to publish books for every reader.

Tarcher and Perigee are registered trademarks, and the colophon is a trademark
of Penguin Random House LLC.

Most TarcherPerigee books are available at special quantity discounts for bulk
purchase for sales promotions, premiums, fund-raising, and educational needs.
Special books or book excerpts also can be created to fit specific needs. For
details, write: SpecialMarkets@penguinrandomhouse.com.

ISBN 9780399183898

Printed in the United States of America
1   3   5   7   9   10   8   6   4   2

Book design by Katy Riegel

I dedicate this book to a person who, when I was a depressed and confused young man, showed me I had a purpose in this world— that I could become a writer. He will never read this dedication because he has since passed away, but his name is Dr. Wayne Dyer.

I'll always remember a story he told that you may be able to relate to. One day, when he was a kid, he went home after school and asked his foster mother, "What's a scurvy elephant?" The woman said, "Huh? Who said that?" Little Wayne told her that his teacher called him a "scurvy elephant." She was so shocked that she went back to the teacher to ask what it was all about. The teacher said, "No! I said Wayne is a 'disturbing element,' not a 'scurvy elephant.'"

In honor of Dr. Dyer, this book is dedicated to all the scurvy elephants out there, to people who are doing things differently, and to those who are bringing more joy to their work and the world.

✳

ACKNOWLEDGMENTS

Whether we know each other or not, I'm well aware that your time is very valuable—there are a million other things you could be doing besides reading this book. I'm also aware that there are a million other ways you could spend your money. So if you choose to, thank you very much for reading my book.

If this is the first time you've been introduced to me or my work, I want to thank you from the bottom of my heart for picking up and considering purchasing *Profit from Happiness*.

Life is impossible on our own, and a book is no different. There are pages of people I could thank, and I do my best to let them know how grateful I am on a regular basis. If you're one of them, I thank you for your being a part of my life.

CONTENTS

INTRODUCTION

How to Be
an Everyday Hero from
Nine to Five and Beyond

THE SECRETS TO winning were forgotten when the game was started. Thousands of years ago, as man began to build economies and maximize economic prosperity, a goal was created: win the game. What game? The game of growth, numbers, prosperity, business, economic expansion, social status, personal freedom, and what would eventually be called "the American dream."

The game was created with the intention to win: to live the good life, to have a nice retirement, to gain as much material and economic reward as possible, and perhaps even to buy a yacht one day. The game was created with the goal of infinite economic growth. More for everyone. The intention was to set records and then break them—to climb the ladder of success.

Minds were filled with dreams of infinite profit and income. Wall Street was paved and businesses were born. We began to construct commercial industries, institutions, and cities. Stocks rose and became a way to measure success in the game. Winning ensured you'd gain more money, power, possessions, and freedom.

The economy soared. People worked hard for its progress; they worked their way toward the promise of freedom and prosperity. Hours worked were reflected in paychecks, and annual income steadily skyrocketed. People became richer than ever before.

These people celebrated as numbers grew and fortunes were made. Land was amassed and statues were erected. Houses were designed and business plans were sketched. Retirement strategies were tailored and investment opportunities appeared—savings accounts grew. People set out to get their share of good fortune and to find success.

And they did. Then the cost of living jumped tenfold; people needed stable jobs and logged more hours at work for extra pay. But it was okay because people were still winning, earning, obtaining, and succeeding.

Then, one day, the bubble burst—the Great Depression came. People lost everything and businesses fell apart. Fortunes folded and money lost its value. It returned to its original form—paper.

Eventually the economy was reborn—labor increased and money trees grew again. It wasn't long before the buildings grew even taller and more intricate. Cities expanded and people competed for jobs and opportunities to work. People wanted to win. Businesses wanted to succeed.

And they did. Profits soared so high that the wolves of Wall Street howled at the full moon of opportunity. People buckled down, worked hard, and logged most of their waking hours working. And they were rewarded. They earned material possessions, big savings, comfort, and security.

Winning was measured by rankings, stocks, ticker symbols, numbers, profit margins, and income. Today we watch those scoreboards as we continue to play the game. The world carries on the tradition of growth, expansion, and opportunity. We want to win. We check the scoreboards to see if we are ahead or behind. We count the numbers and log in the hours each week, even if we don't want to be there.

The numbers are clear: according to a Gallup survey, 71 percent of workers are disengaged at work. Adults employed full time in the United States report working an average of forty-seven hours per week, almost a full workday longer than a standard five-day, nine-to-five schedule entails. Around three-quarters of us are spending most of our waking hours doing something we do not like or care about. This may explain why there is ten times more major depression in people born after 1945 than in those born before, in just a half century of playing the game. And today two million Americans quit their jobs every month, not because the jobs don't pay well, but because people don't like them and don't feel empowered in the workplace.

It looks like we're playing the game in the wrong way. Whether we believe it or not, we are losing the work-and-money game. We've put so much emphasis on getting things done, on finishing to-do lists, on growth, and on economic demand, that we're beginning to lose—big time.

While annual income has soared over the past sixty years, happiness has stayed the same. And although the United States is one of the wealthiest countries in the world, in happiness it scores below fifteen other developed nations. Where is Marvin Gaye to sing so beautifully, "Hey! What's going on?"

We believed that we could continue to win if we kept our heads down and worked until our eyes fell out. We thought it was okay to feel unfulfilled as long as we kept showing up for work and getting everything done as best we could. Only now are we realizing that this is actually having a negative effect on productivity in the workplace.

Many companies are beginning to lose lots of money, because when people aren't happy they aren't focused, energized, empowered, or efficient. When energy is low, so is effort and effectiveness. That's why, according to Gallup, the US economy absorbs approximately $500 billion a year in productivity losses because employees feel disengaged, disempowered, and unfulfilled.

We've always believed that the rules of the game were work and growth at all costs. And now we're seeing that there is actually a price we can't continue to pay: we're unhappy and we're losing money because of it. Results flow where energy goes. And if the energy is not there, if we are not emotionally connected and stimulated or finding fulfillment, then we have no firepower. We are not energized, and we have no real happiness or connection to anything that matters to us.

This causes us to lose the game on all levels. It's bad for us as individuals, because the whole point of work is to provide for ourselves and our loved ones, and to be happy. We're working more than ever, but we're less happy than ever. And businesses, nations, and economies are losing money because of it too. The economy is broken. The days add up and people are tired. Somehow we keep showing up, but we aren't getting the results we could if we felt more fulfilled.

"Just keep pushing," we tell ourselves. "If I work hard enough, I'll get a bonus." We believe we will get that house, car, suit, or dress we really want. Many of us think that when our money is stacked high enough, happiness will be restored. But nothing has proven to be further from the truth. This is not to say that money isn't important—it is. Money can take you from stress into comfort. It can buy some freedom. It can give you a comfortable place to live and help you support your loved ones. But at a certain point, something else needs to drive us. In fact, a 2010 Princeton University study by Daniel Kahneman and Angus Deaton found that, at the national level, making more than $75,000 per year won't significantly improve your day-to-day happiness.

But somehow we continue to run through the motions, nearly working ourselves to death. The secrets to winning big time remain secret. That's because we've been operating under the assumption that happiness and fulfillment do not enhance productivity and success. We've been playing the game by the wrong rules, falsely believing that we win by sacrificing well-being for work.

We've been missing some basic facts, like the *Harvard Business Review*'s findings that satisfied employees have 31 percent higher productivity, generate 37 percent more sales, and are three times more creative than their disengaged counterparts. Or Gallup's discoveries that the top 25 percent of engaged workers have 50 percent fewer accidents, as well as significantly lower health costs.

The game has reached a tipping point: we've begun to realize that we can no longer increase the number of hours and the amount of stress we put on people to raise their levels of productivity. What we're finding is that if we want to see what people are capable of achieving, we have to create new definitions of happiness and leadership, both in and out of work.

Our work must energize, empower, enliven, and stimulate us. This secret to finding personal fulfillment, success, and productivity has been forgotten, and we have to find it again. If our daily tasks or overall objectives at work aren't fulfilling, and the money we earn doesn't give us that feeling, then what will bring us happiness and fulfillment? We need to find the answer to this question so we can win the game. Besides, the happier we are, the better we perform.

So the real question is: what makes us happy? A great book, *All In: How the Best Managers Create a Culture of Belief and Drive Big Results* by Adrian Gostick and Chester Elton, shows evidence that happy workers are more productive. However, the authors do not use those exact words. Instead of "happy," they describe workers as "energized, engaged, and enabled." They call their version of happiness "the three Es":

- Energized: you feel a sense of well-being and drive.
- Engaged: you're attached to your work and willing to put in extra effort.

■ Enabled: your work environment supports your productivity and performance. You are empowered.

If we break down what we mean by happiness, we usually find that it involves these feelings of being energized, enabled, empowered, and stimulated. We are happy when we feel seen and heard, when we feel that we are in the proper place at the proper time and feeling good.

This book focuses on practical ways of obtaining happiness, growing our income through fulfillment, on feeling inspired to go to work, feeling valued and stimulated during the day, and feeling fulfilled in our personal lives when we return home. This is not some crazy, idealized notion. In fact, there is no other alternative for many of us. We deserve to win the game, and it is inevitable that we will continue to play it. A good number of us work most of the years of our lives, and we should feel a sense of fulfillment in our work. We are doing ourselves a disservice by perpetuating a society where the majority of people would like to quit their jobs.

Either we keep doing what we've always done and receive what we've always received (depression, unhappiness, low productivity, lack of focus, and loss of money), or we try something new. Viktor E. Frankl survived the Nazi concentration camps and found meaning in the midst of his incredible struggle. He wrote that "life is never made unbearable by circumstances, only by lack of meaning and purpose . . . when we are no longer able to change a situation, we are challenged to change ourselves."

I'd like to suggest that if Frankl could find meaning, connection, purpose, and inner peace in some of the worst circumstances a person could imagine, then certainly we can find more fulfillment, connection, meaning, stimulation, success, and productivity in the workplace.

Our biology hasn't changed in fifty thousand years, but our environment certainly has. Today's workplaces tend to be full of stress, cynicism, disconnection, and self-interest. They are often not what we want them to be. But Viktor Frankl has shown us something wonderful—the best organizations and happiest people are not always the ones who have the best circumstances. No matter what cards we are dealt, no matter what we think we're missing or have lost, there's one thing we—as a person, team, or organization— can never lose: the freedom to choose our focus and attitude in any set of circumstances. Everybody needs the freedom to find the path of least resistance and to do the things that innately fulfill them as human beings. Even at a job we are not absolutely passionate about, we can find energy, empowerment, and personal fulfillment during the hours of nine to five and beyond.

If you're reading this, chances are you and I are similar in that we have the means to live but no guaranteed meaning to live for. The problem is that we've been putting our energy into things that do not make us happy. And when we do not find happiness, we often think we must change our environment. But I'd like to propose that what we're actually being called to do is to become so powerful that we can find happiness in our current work and life environments. To do this we need to stop focusing on how little care, empowerment, and stimulation we feel from others and start focusing on our own potential to increase the amount of care and support we provide to the people in our lives. This is where happiness is created. This quality is the mark of a leader and the definition of an everyday hero.

Your job title, life story, and whether you've been considered a leader don't matter. It's time we all become leaders. It's time we all become everyday heroes—people who live their lives to care about and nurture positive connections with those around them. Today we must all become leaders who create the kind of workplaces and home environments that will help those around us bloom into everyday heroes too.

When more people feel seen, heard, appreciated, and cared for, productivity and personal fulfillment increase hand in hand. We see a drop in the number of people who are depressed. We see profit margins rise. We feel more meaning and more connection to our life and work experiences, no matter how mundane and unpleasant they seemed before. Sometimes you can't necessarily change the cards you've been dealt, but you can change how you look at them and play with them.

WHERE SHOULD PEOPLE place the most emphasis as they show up to work and in life each day? How can they reap the most benefits from their efforts? The answer is connection. Connection is why we are here. It's what gives purpose and meaning to our lives. The ability to feel connected is neurobiological and is what stimulates us. Connection to ourselves, to our lives, to meaning, and to others is what energizes, empowers, and enables us.

We need to focus more on the things that make us better people, and this book will help you do that. This book will give you the tools to transform yourself into an everyday hero. An everyday hero is someone who lives by these six creeds:

- give to get
- share a smile
- step outside yourself
- lend an ear
- don't take anything personally
- stay open and vulnerable

When individuals engage in their work in ways that help others, and find meaning in daily circumstances and interactions (even when they seem monotonous), they are more energized, engaged, and empowered. They are more motivated and they are happier. They find higher levels of success, engagement, productivity, and meaning. They are of more value. The challenge is for us, as individuals, to find ways to craft our everyday interactions, during the nine-to-five hours and beyond, so we have well-connected relationships, more chances to find our significance, more opportunities to create value by helping others, and more visible impact from what we do.

You need a very strong will to successfully adopt these six creeds and change your mind-set. If you can, you will become an everyday hero inside and outside the workplace. You will need focus to improve the energy of your organization, home, or life, but if you can begin to live your life with these principles in mind, your transformation will be amazing. The improvement in your productivity, inspiration, and engagement at work will be astounding. Your leadership abilities will skyrocket. You will inspire others and see more joy and connection in their eyes when you come around. You will be more valued and appreciated by those around you.

If you can manage to live by these six creeds, you will see the drama and stress of your work and personal life disappear before your very eyes. Instead of living in an uninspired and unfulfilled state during your workdays and weekends, or feeling half-energized, you will help create a world that enthuses you. You will feel grateful to be alive and will wake up with joy each day—and you will make more money as a result.

You can do this simply by changing your focus. Becoming an everyday hero is just a matter of making small changes each day. I urge you to log the time you consistently show up in your work and life in the ways this book illustrates, and watch as you profit, in myriad ways, from your personal growth.

CREED ONE

Give to Get

IF YOU ARE reading this, you probably wouldn't mind increasing your health, wealth, and happiness. It wouldn't be a bad thing, would it? People have been taught to believe that if you sacrifice enough, you will become rich and, as a result, will find happiness. However, when we look back over the years, we may see that we've become richer but not happier.

What's the catch? We've worked hard, we really have, but how has it turned out for us? Today the paradigm is shifting so you can actually make the money you dream of making *and* become a happier, more valuable human being—in life and the workplace—not by working the most hours at your job, but by offering the most value as a person.

You get what you give. Do you want a greater flow of

money, happiness, joy, kindness, fulfillment, or success? Then you must increase your value to the world and those around you.

One of the first things we must consider is that money and happiness are energy. To create a steadily increasing stream of money, we can't view it as merely a material entity but need to think of it as an expression of energy—ultimately, of our own energy. When we stop growing, it stops growing. When we are of less value, we earn less in return.

Wealth has an easily predictable energy flow. If we imagine an increasing flow of money, we don't see a stationary, material object, do we? No. We think of continuous growth and movement—movement beyond what is or what has been, to unknown and perhaps only dreamed of heights. We do not think of limits and finite goals but of ongoing progress and expansion toward infinity. To connect with this, we have to be that way ourselves. We do this by continuously growing as people, by becoming more valuable to the world. The power to create money, success, and happiness of all kinds comes in direct proportion to our ability to become more than we currently are—our ability to expand our value and potential and increase our own energy. Money, which is an extension of our personal energy, will follow in proportion to our own personal growth.

There has never been a better time to increase your value,

find more happiness, and make more money as a result. This is because the marketplace is in desperate need of your growth, leadership, value, personality, and positive attitude. Don't believe me? Then why, as I mentioned before, does the US economy lose about $500 billion a year due to lack of productivity? The marketplace suffers because people are not inspired or happy and therefore not as productive as they could be.

So what's the solution? We need to find people who will work more productively. How do we do that? Send all the work to China? Pay motivational speakers a bunch of money to fire people up? No! (Although, you can pay me if you want.) We need to develop a society and workplace with better leaders and better human beings, who offer more value to those around them.

The key word is "value." It's important to know a few attributes that factor into your increased value in the marketplace: leadership, quality, attitude, and quantity. How well do you work with others? How much do you empower them? Are you a leader? If so, what kind? Do you have a positive attitude? How much value do you deliver in terms of your skill set? How many people are you impacting?

When Justine Musk—the first wife of billionaire Elon Musk (net worth $11.4 billion), who is the founder of PayPal, CEO of Tesla Motors, SpaceX, and chairman of

SolarCity—was asked, "Will I become a billionaire if I am determined to be one and put in all the necessary work required?" she answered, "No."

She explained that this is not the right question to ask: "You're determined. So what? Shift your focus away from what you want [a billion dollars] and get deeply, intensely curious about what the world wants and needs. Ask yourself what you have the potential to offer that is so unique and compelling and helpful that no computer could replace you, no one could outsource you . . . then develop that potential. . . . The world doesn't throw a billion dollars at a person because the person wants it or works hard. [The world does not care what you want.] The world gives you money in exchange for something it perceives to be of equal or greater value."

In my work, I often travel around the world and speak to companies. Before the speeches begin, the people who hire me give me a breakdown of the organization and always point out the most valuable players (MVPs). "We're having a lot of problems with leadership, which is why we brought you in. There's not much connection and interaction between team members," they often say. "People aren't inspired to work."

"Well, who's your MVE—your most valuable energy?" I reply. Never once in my experience has the person who logged the most hours and been considered the most valuable player also been the one with the most valuable energy. Often the best workers have been the worst people to deal with—that is, they have the worst energy. That's why I believe it's important to realize that we're in a crisis when it comes to two important resources: the first is leadership, and the second is positive energy. Most things are replaceable, but real leadership, positive energy, and true interest in other human beings are not.

Why do I bring up the term "most valuable energy"? Because everything is energy! Whether it's the sun, an idea, art, money, or an organization—it's energy. If our MVPs are transmitting bad energy, no wonder so many people hate their jobs and their bosses! If the leadership of a company has stagnating energy, it is destined to create disgruntled employees and lack of productivity.

Why is it (as I've found) that the best workers often have the most dysfunctional teams? I think it's because we haven't quite grasped that there are more important things than sitting at your desk and working in silence. Each interaction we have with others gives us an opportunity to improve or harm the energy and the atmosphere of the relationship. To truly succeed together, we must work on ourselves and our relationships as much as, and even more than, our work. This means becoming a better human being, not just logging the most hours on the job.

At the end of the day, you can't buy loyalty: you have

to earn it. That's why most people don't like their bosses and why companies overinvest in leadership training that doesn't work. Everyone must lead by example. The only way to earn loyalty and to have an inspired family, organization, or society is by becoming a leader yourself—not a tunnel-visioned worker.

Well, what about Steve Jobs? you may ask. Many people say he was nasty, but he still built an empire! That may be true. There are times for tough love, but in today's world we need more heart. Besides, Apple did not think the value of Steve Jobs's work outweighed his inability to be a compassionate leader with positive energy, so they got rid of him. And he did not come back around for his second try until he was humbled into change.

People need to feel seen, heard, respected, and empowered. People are finally beginning to realize that there are more important things than occasionally lucking into success with a guy like Jobs. By and large, people are less productive and less inspired when they have nasty leaders. People do not show up in full for those who do not respect, see, and empower them. Today the world needs more people who lead with their hearts. The person who makes everyone feel valued has an attribute with a limitless ceiling for potential monetary return.

Making the money you want, becoming the person you choose to be, and feeling the happiness you desire do not have to be separate pursuits. You don't have to choose one or the other. They can work as a team. You can have them all.

About three years ago, I dreamed of becoming a writer and public speaker. I thought that would make me happy. The problem wasn't that I didn't have something that mattered to me; the problem was that I wasn't making any money. No money at all. I booked about thirty speaking gigs around my first book release. I was so excited, until I found out how much money I would (not) make: five hundred dollars. No, not five hundred dollars for each appearance; five hundred dollars in total! I did twenty-nine speaking engagements for zero dollars and one for five hundred! If it wasn't for in-person book sales at those events, I wouldn't have had enough money to drive to the next speech. If it wasn't for the generous people who booked me and also let me stay in their guest rooms, I'd have been homeless on my out-of-state tour. I was also operating under the fallacy that I needed to work harder to make money—I logged more and more hours, gave more and more speeches, drove even more miles, and lost my health. I was in the worst shape of my life. I was skinnier, weaker, slower, and less flexible than I'd ever been. To top it all off, I was making just enough to avoid being in debt and to continue living on the road with zero expenses.

I was on a hamster wheel: I needed a gig almost every day because I needed a bed for the night, because I couldn't afford a hotel. I was stuck—and it stunk! How could I deliver value when I was losing my health and happiness in the process? When this happens, it's usually time to ask a few questions like, what do I do? In my case, I stumbled across a YouTube video of business philosopher Jim Rohn speaking about how he went from being a miserable, unhealthy, in-debt twenty-five-year-old to a millionaire by the time he was thirty. He explained that everything changed for him when *he* changed.

You can't change your surroundings and pry more money out of people. Well, you can, but you'll probably be fired or put in jail or simply find yourself out of luck sooner or later. You can't go to your closet and grab some happiness. But you can have more wealth and happiness if you learn to give more of the valuable parts of yourself.

In those early days, I wasn't much of a public speaker. (I guess that's why I was getting paid zero dollars an hour, right?) In fact, I started doing it only because I learned that if I put a book out, it wouldn't automatically sell a million copies. I had to go out and champion the message myself. And unfortunately for me, I didn't know a lot about, or have much experience in, the art of speaking, inspiring, leading, or writing. But I knew it was what I wanted to do; I just wanted to be able to make more money at it and be happier.

The first thing I learned from Rohn is that we don't

actually get paid for our time. We get paid for the value we deliver, according to the marketplace. *Value*, not time. Many people think, "I make thirty dollars an hour." But then you break it down and thirty dollars per hour isn't exactly true. If it were true, we could stay home, eat pizza, have a party in our favorite pajamas, dance the night away, and wait for our check. And that isn't the case, is it? No.

You actually get paid for value. You don't get paid for the hour—you get paid for the value you put into that hour. Why does one guitar teacher cost fifty dollars an hour, while an hour-long lesson with Carlos Santana would be unaffordable for most people? Well, because Santana delivers more value in that hour than the average guitar teacher does. Why can one massage therapist charge thirty-five dollars an hour and another a hundred and fifty? Because people pay more for higher-quality work. Why does one motivational speaker get paid five hundred dollars for a sixty-minute keynote speech, while Jack Welch gets upward of fifty thousand dollars for that same hour? Because Jack Welch puts more value into the hour.

Look around at most rich people. Chances are they did not steal their money. Chances are they did not get rich through brute force or luck. Why does Steve Wozniak (cofounder of Apple) have so much money? Because Jobs and Wozniak added tremendous value to the modern age.

Do you see what I mean? It's ultimately the value you

give that determines the money you receive. It definitely takes time to bring that desired value to the marketplace. But it's something that we must learn, because we don't get paid for time.

If you show up at work (or plan to at some point in your life), you probably value money to some degree. Showing up at work means trading your time for money. But this will never set you free. Instead, you must trade your value for money, which will take some time. But there are only so many hours in the day, and there is infinite potential within you. The potential time you can offer for money pales in comparison to the potential value you can offer for it.

Rohn explains that if you become twice as valuable, you can make double the amount of money. It's even possible to become five times as valuable and make five times more money. What about ten times? Yes! It's all possible if we do what Justine Musk suggests: "Shift your focus away from what you want and get deeply, intensely curious about what the world wants and needs. Ask yourself what you have the potential to offer that is so unique and compelling and helpful that you cannot be replaced or outsourced . . . then develop that potential. . . . The world doesn't throw a billion dollars at a person because the person wants it or works hard. The world gives you money in exchange for something it perceives to be of equal or greater value."

Become more valuable and you will earn more. The whole system is a staircase. At the bottom of the stairs you have minimum wage. At the top you have someone like Tim Cook of Apple, Elon Musk, or Oprah Winfrey. They've added a lot of value to the marketplace, haven't they?

In 2011, Tim Cook was compensated $377,996,537. I don't know what his actual income was, but in some form or another the company paid him $377,996,537. If you helped a company make $65 billion, would they pay you $300 million? Absolutely. But why so much? Because that person has become very valuable.

Why do you think Apple pays people at their physical stores close to minimum wage? It's because they are just not as valuable to Apple. They are much more replaceable.

Many people say, "But it's not all about money." And trust me, I know—you're listening to a minimalist hippy here. I'm not saying that it's all about money, but I do think everyone wants to feel valuable and to develop their potential. Why wouldn't you—if you could feel happier and get paid more for it? The truth is that in our reality money plays an important role for most of us. Money problems are the number one cause of divorce. Love, our most treasured resource, is torn apart because of lack of money. And that shouldn't happen! Especially because if you become a better leader—by studying harder; uplifting your energy and the energy of those around you; offering more value, positivity, and compassion to others; listening more closely, smiling more, and transmitting a better attitude—you will not only become more valuable and eventually make more money but chances are you'll save your relationships, marriage, and friendships. You'll ignite them and live them with more passion than you've ever experienced before! You'll uncover a deeper connection to those around you and feel greater love for yourself and this short life. And you'll make more money as a result.

Money is actually the least valuable thing you can earn by living this way. It's not what you can get that matters most but who you can become. Ironically, the greatest value to the marketplace is the value of an individual—you! The bigger you become, the bigger role you play in this life, the happier you will be and the more valuable you will become to the marketplace. It all works together. There's an opportunity of a lifetime to make more money by becoming happier, healthier, and more positive. You become more valuable by being a loving and committed member of the human race.

Some people think, "I'll be patient and wait until I get my raise." But the facts show that it'll happen much faster if you go to work on your value and climb that ladder. You hardly ever get rich or happy by staying in the same place and waiting.

Others say, "Well, I'll just protest." But as Jim Rohn explains, you *never* get rich by demanding it. You make more money and become happier by growing and changing, not by demanding. The idea is to *profit from happiness.* Besides, where's the fun in demanding? The fun is in growing! Why not become more than you've ever been before?

How hard can it be to become a more valuable, unique leader who empowers those around you? Just smile and have a great attitude, say a few kind words, offer to do favors for people around you, and you'll probably earn a few extra bucks pretty quickly.

What if we truly uncover the potential within ourselves? What if we really take it seriously and offer more than we have and become better than we've been? What if we work on being more positive than ever before? How much more health, wealth, and happiness could be ours? How much more money could you make in the next thirty-six months if you really took this seriously?

Remember, it's not the hours worked that determine our pay but the value we put into the hours! So going back to the question, is it possible to become twice as valuable, twice as much of a leader, and make twice the amount of money? Five times? Ten times? Yes! Yes! Yes!

I asked myself this question, and then I had no choice but to get to work. I changed my way of being. I studied my craft and worked hard to become a better example and leader. I learned to communicate more effectively, and I made much more of an effort to be kinder to and more caring with anyone whose path I crossed. I worked with speaking coaches, and I got in the best physical shape of my life. I invested in myself. And at the same time I slowed down and asked people how they were doing. I became more positive. I read a lot more and learned more about how I think. I listened more, smiled more, and gave out better energy to be around. I set intentions and I worked on myself. I didn't know if it was possible to profit from happiness, from giving, and from leadership—from becoming more valuable—but I was curious to find out.

Then January 2015 came around. About two years had passed since my being an excited dreamer had turned into starving misery. My second book was just about to be released, and I received an e-mail. Two e-mails, actually. The first presented me with the opportunity to speak for twenty minutes across the country, and offered to buy almost more books than I had sold in the past two years combined—guaranteed sales! And I could speak in front of fifteen hundred people—more than I had ever spoken to in my entire life!

The second e-mail was from a company that wanted to book me for a gig and pay me more money than I'd made over the past eighteen months! Is this real life? I wondered. They said I wouldn't have to sleep in my car (phew!) or someone's guest room—I would be compensated for a very nice hotel, travel, and food.

That's about the time I got the picture. Wait, what happened? How did I go from making practically zero dollars an hour to making more money than I'd made in my whole life from a single keynote speech?

It's simple: I'd become much more *valuable*. I'd increased my *leadership* and the *care* I showed others. The *quality* of my public speaking had improved—I'd studied and practiced more and was thus in higher demand. I was flat-out better than ever. My *attitude* became more positive as companies began to hire me to help with team building and leadership training. And my value increased in *quantity*—I went from speaking in front of just a few people (if I was lucky) to addressing thousands. And I didn't have to trade in my health, values, or happiness for the cash. They all came together. You can have it all!

Achieving success, making money, becoming a better person, and feeling happiness are really not separable. They're all part of the same process: Become more than you've been, and you can have more than you've had. Stay as you've always been, and you'll get exactly what you've always had.

Remember: *you're paid in direct proportion to the amount of value you add, according to your work and the marketplace.* Increase your value, offer more, become more as a person, and with time you will earn more money. You don't need to wait for a new boss, economy, or government. You are the key to your better future.

Anything is possible when we understand how to get what we want. If you want more kindness, give it. If you want more money, offer more value. If you want more love, love. If you want more leaders around, become one. If you do this, you will have it all. The first step toward any change is to understand that you cannot have what you want until you deliver equal or more value to those around you.

CREED ONE

- Instead of asking yourself how to get what you want, ask yourself: How can I give equal or greater value? How can I increase my value at work and/or in the marketplace? What's my plan to do it?
- Write down the amount of money you want. Next to it write out the amount of value you will give for it—in specifics. Not, "I will give a lot of value," but specifically how you will generate more value in your work, to those around you, and/or in the marketplace.
- Another way to look at this is, how can I give the thing I want to get? Like Justine Musk said: shift your focus away from the thing you want to how you can deliver value. When you shift your mind-set away from what you can get and focus instead on how you can offer value, you will be rewarded for your efforts. So instead of thinking about doubling your income, ask yourself, how can I double my value at work or in the marketplace?

Share a Smile

How often do you ask people "How's it going?" and hear responses like "Busy!" "So busy!" "Too busy!" followed by a sigh? What puzzles me is that this frantic busyness is often not necessary. This is not the response we usually hear from someone who works eighteen-hour shifts, six days a week, to feed their kids. Nor from a woman who walks ten miles a day to transport clean water on her head so her family doesn't die of dehydration. And we don't hear it from that guy in Detroit who walked twenty miles to work every day (sunshine, rain, or snow) for the past twenty years. We don't because these people don't have time to tell you they're busy.

America's average busyness is created by people who take on tasks that are not a matter of life and death. They seem like a matter of life and death, but they are not. This busyness is a choice: work, school, hobbies. People are busy because they are addicted to it—because they are afraid to face what would be left in its absence.

Almost everyone I know is busy, and if they're not busy, they feel anxious or guilty about their free time. They rush through their work, their conversations, and their personal lives. There are just so many things to do! The day is planned out from the moment the alarm clock rings at six thirty to the time they lay their heads back on the pillow. But this busyness is a problem—it gives us no time for connection with others, which is what makes us happy.

Is it possible that when we feel anxious, cranky, and sad it's actually a symptom of an overly competitive world—a world driven by the desire for productivity regardless of the costs? It's a likely possibility. Look around: too many people are depressed. No one wants to live like this. It's something we collectively and passive-aggressively force one another to do. Get busy, get going! What does this rushed existence amount to in the end? Depression. Stress. Unhappiness. Regret. Ulcers. Suicide. Fear. Hypertension. Addiction.

Have you ever wondered if all this busyness could be a way to cover up the fact that most of what we do doesn't actually matter? We may be busy, but what exactly is getting done? While we are hustling down the hallway, worried about crossing everything off our lists, are we making the days of those around us (or our own, for that matter) better? Are we making ourselves or anyone else around us happy? Are we creating a beautiful and meaningful life?

We use busyness to reassure us that life isn't empty. We convince ourselves that it's okay that we are not living beautiful or meaningful lives, because we are busy. We tell ourselves that because we are so busy, we do not have the time to connect with the person in the hallway, or to create a genuine conversation with the cashier at the store. Life can't possibly be a waste of time if we're so busy all the time . . . right? Wrong. The rush is a vain attempt to drown out the big-picture questions that we keep at bay. Questions like: What is the meaning of my life? Am I happy? Am I actually being a good person or just a busy person?

I can't answer those questions for you, but I can give you one tip: slow down and smile. Even if you don't like the current state of your life, smiling will still help. It makes you and those around you happier. It creates the opportunity for beautiful and meaningful moments.

Even if you are sad inside and don't feel like smiling, a fake smile can help. Your neurotransmitters and endorphins are not biased: they could care less if you fake a smile or not. They just want you to smile so they can fire in your brain and make you feel good. The brain doesn't seem to differentiate between real or fake; it interprets the position of the facial muscles in the same way whether they happen spontaneously or are put on. This is known as the "facial feedback hypothesis." The more we stimulate the brain to release these chemicals, the more often we feel happy and relaxed.

Remember that everything is energy—you are energy, I am energy. So when you smile at the people whose paths you cross (even when you're so busy that you think you don't have time to be happy), your neurotransmitters trigger not only your own endorphins but theirs. And even when your bottom line is simply to get things done, getting those endorphins pumping will help you finish your work faster and better—I assure you.

It doesn't make sense to believe that to succeed in life we must sacrifice feeling happy and connected. Your brain works better when it's stimulated by endorphins, and endorphins are released when you are happy. Happiness is ignited by smiling, which in turn makes others feel good.

All this is within your control. It's not dependent on whether you make enough sales, receive good news, buy a nice car, or if people are nice to you or you wake up on the right side of the bed—it's contingent on your decision to share a smile, not only with yourself, but also with others.

As soon as we are too busy to share a smile—to curve our lips in a jolly way—we've lost. If we work to improve the quality of our lives but sacrifice smiling and making other people happy, which is the most basic and impor-

22

tant form of happiness, we are digging ourselves a grave. We become the walking dead.

Imagine if someone said to you, "Okay, you're going to grow up, get a job, live your life, and try to be as busy as possible . . . and you will never have time to stop and smile because then you will fall behind." If you heard this stated so bluntly, you would never accept such a future—yet we do, and many of us live like this every day.

I look into people's eyes throughout the day and feel that they wish they could scream, just let it all out. But instead, deep within, they wait for something to make them happy—a paycheck, a movie, ice cream, exercise, sex, something they can buy—anything to release the craziness of life.

But I'm telling you that you could be much happier than you are now without having to buy or change anything—just by smiling at people more often. Just by becoming that "crazy" person who never quits grinning. Why not? Smiling is synonymous with happiness, part and parcel with the good life, so why don't we do it? Why do we have to wait for something or someone to make us smile? We don't have to. And it's much easier than putting all our focus into being number one and working ourselves to the bone. We don't have to sacrifice everything to get there, only to find out that it amounts to nothing in the end.

The biggest fallacy is that in order to achieve success we

need to log as many hours as possible and stay endlessly occupied. In fact, this costs us everything in the end. People who have seemingly good lives commit suicide in situations like this. Yes, even people who make good money and who are productive commit suicide because they can't take it anymore.

If we changed nothing other than smiling one hundred times more often than we normally do, all our lives would be greatly affected. Even if the person you smile at doesn't smile back, you are making a difference. I bet we would make more money, be more productive, and go to sleep with a deeper sense of confidence and meaning if we were just in the habit of looking people genuinely in the eyes and smiling at them. We work ourselves to the bone to feel a sense of purpose and significance. We want to feel valued. And we all know that we feel good when we make others feel good. But you don't need to start a charity to give—just start smiling.

I can't tell you how many times I've had a bad day, or at least thought I was having one, and then someone smiled at me and it brought me back to my center. It's like a jolt of reality that clears my mind and puts me at ease. In fact, last week I was walking back from the gym in Hollywood late at night on a dark, unlit street. I'm a small-town beach boy, so sometimes I feel edgy or unsafe in a big city. As I walked, I came to a homeless encampment. I saw, out of the corner of my eye, a homeless guy standing there, looking at me. I stepped off the sidewalk and walked in the gutter because I was sure he was either going to ask me for money or mug me. I wanted to avoid him at all costs. Meanwhile I continued to worry about work and other things.

I walked with my head down, suffering about money, career goals, and unmet expectations. I was confined in the narrow parameters I'd set in my small mind: expectations about myself and judgments about this homeless guy. At best, I thought, he'll take ten seconds of my time and ask for money. At worst, he'll mug me. At any rate, he'll distract me from worrying about money and my Facebook "Likes."

Then a car's blue headlights came toward me. I didn't want to be run over, so I had no choice but to step back onto the sidewalk, closer to the man I was sure was going to prey on me. I kept looking down at the sidewalk, as if the littered ground had the beauty I yearned for, as if it would give me the sense of aliveness I'm ultimately after.

I started to worry that I would trip over the curb in the darkness, fall into the street, get hit by the car, and die. So I had no choice but to look up to see where I was going. Still, I tried to avoid eye contact at all costs. And then there was this face, looking at me, five feet away, with no teeth in his mouth, smiling as wide as the hole in my heart, perhaps even wider. "Have a great night!" said the man, while sharing his huge smile.

I stared at his toothless grin, and before I could even think, my mouth opened into a smile too. It was like a black hole spinning in endless space, opening out of nowhere, and sucking away all my thoughts, worries, and questions. Everything was erased. I hung, suspended in space, in ecstasy, in connection with myself, with another person, with happiness. Time froze. I was happy. I realized that *this* is the feeling I am after. When this happens, all my anxiety is gone. It will still be there if I want to go back to it, but for this moment it's gone. I feel like I know why I'm alive—I remember that I'm here to connect, share, appreciate, and smile, simply because I can.

What seemed like forever was only a moment. I took another step and then the face of the man who lived on the street, who gave me happiness, was gone. I kept walking, and the feeling was still there. I was still smiling. I was happy.

My problems seemed less important. It made me think: Why do I waste time living in my head when life is happening in front of me? Why don't I take a breath and smile just because I can? It makes me feel way better than worrying about things I can't control. And let's face it—most of our worries are things we can't actually control. You can't control the way your parent or your boss or your significant other is acting. Nor can you control the economy when it is running amok. And worrying about things, especially about getting things done, is not going to get you to the top faster or make you feel happier. The top is here, in this moment, waiting for you to let someone into your heart. I know it can be hard because we've all been hurt and let down—life has hard moments. People can be strange and cruel, life can be unpredictable, and times can be tough. But what's the worst that can happen if you slow down for a second and smile? I mean genuinely smile. Not one of those half-a-second, did-anyone-notice-me? smiles. Not an I'm-busy, I-don't-really-have-time-for-you, I'm-more-important smile. Not an I'll-make-eye-contact-with-you-for-a-brief-second-and-tell-you-my-day-is-good-even-though-it-isn't smile. I'm talking about a true, genuine smile.

Seriously? What's the worst that can happen? Will you lose your job because you took five seconds to smile? If that's the case, you need a different job. Will people think you're crazy because you're happy? If so, forget them. This is about you and your life, not their thoughts. It's better to appear strange to others than to be a stranger to yourself.

Usually we think the worst that can happen to us is that we'll become broke, fat, sick, and ugly. That's the judgment I made about the homeless guy. I thought he was worthless, broke, homeless, fat, ugly, and perhaps even sick. But is ending up like that guy the worst that can happen? Is he really poor if he can make someone else's life better? Is he actually poor if he's able to wish someone a good day, be happy, share love, and be of value? That's what he was for me. And that's what we all want, right? To be happy. To be of value. To feel love. To have a good day. To make people smile.

Where does fulfillment of those desires come from? I can assure you that it doesn't start in an expressionless, robotic face that shares neither happiness nor disdain. I can assure you that the fulfillment you crave won't come from being famous on social media or from your dream house. And it won't come from being a movie star—just ask the Hollywood celebrities in rehab. Nor will it come from millions of dollars or being on top of the corporate world—just ask the families of the megamillion executives who commit suicide every year because they are confused and depressed.

The secret our culture has forgotten is that everything we could ever want is here now. You just need to have the courage to claim it. It's scary because it's hard to be alone. It's hard to do something that no one else seems to be doing. It's hard to say: You know what? I may be having a bad day, I may have enough stress for a whole village of people to be anxious, I may have a zillion things to do, but I have time to smile because I am alive! I am on a rock spinning through space. That last thought alone should put us in a state of ecstasy, on the verge of crying, laughing, and peeing our pants from too much happiness to control.

Living like this *is* possible. It starts with a choice, which eventually becomes a habit. We need to make a habit of connecting, looking people in the eyes, and smiling. And of answering with a truthful response when someone asks how our day was.

You may think, well, I don't have enough energy to do that. I used to tell myself that one a lot: "I don't have the energy to stop everything I am doing and smile for four seconds. I don't have the energy to talk to that person and ask them how their day is and spend fifteen seconds seeing if I can make them smile. I don't have the energy."

Really, you don't have the energy? You *are* energy! You are trillions of pulsating cells vibrating so fast that they appear as a solid body to our limited senses. And you are sharing that energy all the time. Whether through stress or freedom, love or hate, confidence or doubt, you are always exuding energy.

Why not choose to give positive energy? Do you think it's childish or something? All we need to do is look around for a minute at the grown-ups: they run around like chickens with their heads cut off (or like my high school's basketball coach used to say when he was very angry, "like heads with their chickens cut off"). We are stuck in our heads, and it's leaving us with a shockingly high national depression rate. We're one of the richest countries in the world and yet we're not the happiest, by far.

People say the best way to learn is to travel. I did that. I took a backpack and wandered around the world, going to villages in Central America where no tourists had ever been. I know this because the locals told me that everyone was staring at me because no outsiders had ever come to their concrete-shack villages. I went to places that I was told never to go. I wandered around from Central America to Southeast Asia.

During my travels, I saw a bunch of people whom Americans would call dirt poor. Nothing we would ever want to become. People without TVs, plumbing, refrigerators, retirement plans, career paths, money, designer clothing, diamond rings, Rolexes, cars, or bus passes. Just eight-by-eight-foot concrete rooms that families of five sleep in and called home.

I would sit cross-legged on the concrete floor while they cooked in their version of a kitchen—a corner of the concrete shack with a little fire. "Dinner!" they would say, while they passed me a plate. "Mmm! What's this?" I would ask. "Coconut-fried cow and fresh fish. It still has the eyes, you see?"

I looked at their kids, who had worn the same clothes the whole week I'd known them. Their shoes had holes and they'd outgrown them, but that didn't stop them from heading out after dinner to play soccer with a flat ball on a barren dirt field. I looked at them all. They smiled from ear to ear. I felt loved like never before. I felt alive like I'd never been. I felt that I had finally figured out what life is about.

Sharing a smile, sharing your vibe—it's your superpower! At least it was these children's superpower. It's what made me feel like they were the happiest people I'd ever met. And I know many millionaires. I am friends with numerous *New York Times* bestselling authors and famous actors. I've dined with billionaires twice. But the greatest privilege I've had was to sit with the people who were in a place in their lives that we would consider a complete failure. Broke. No electricity. No fine dining. No chance to make real money. No way to fill up their schedule. And yet all the time in the world to remember that life is about love, happiness, and smiling just because you are alive.

We often think, "I'm not happy, therefore I can't smile," when, in reality, we're not happy because we don't take the time to smile. Or we think, "That's just my disposition—I don't smile much," when, in reality, our nature is to smile. And some think, "This is all great, but I have bills to pay, a business to build." And that's exactly why so many businesses fail. That's exactly why the United States loses $550 billion to low productivity a year. That's exactly why motivational speakers get $50,000 to talk to corporations for an hour, in hopes of inspiring them to work harder and achieve more.

We're caught in the suffocating belief that everything else can wait but now we have to work. When, in reality, if everyone at your workplace smiled at one another more often we would actually spark a new kind of atmosphere. A place where people would be inspired to go to work and companies would be more profitable than ever. Our dopamine and endorphin receptors would be more active, and people would naturally be happier. They would be in better moods, and they would have better mental clarity and focus. We would be fulfilling our innate psychological needs for connection, feeling of value, and smiling.

Just smile, real quick. Seriously, just stop reading for one second and turn your mouth up into the curve of all things jolly. Now smile at someone else. Smile as much as possible and see what happens.

CREED TWO

- Put this book on your lap. Close your eyes and smile really big. Seriously! Just hold your smile. Don't wait for something to make you smile. Just smile because you can and because it makes you feel good. Do it for thirty seconds. Then go find someone and make them smile. Notice that this brings joy and a sense of meaning to life—to smile and to make others smile.

CREED THREE

Step Outside Yourself

IF I TOLD you that in the future you were going to wake up every morning and sit at your desk, in front of your computer, solving problems and answering e-mails and talking to no one unless you needed something from them, would you want to do it? Probably not. You'd probably say, "No way. I need to interact and connect with people. That sounds awful!" Yet this is what a lot of us do every day.

Oftentimes, the only reason we turn to anyone during the day is that we need something—only, in other words, when it is for our own personal benefit. We rarely step outside what we're doing simply to help someone else, and this leaves us feeling unmotivated and unfulfilled. This is one of my qualms with the self-help industry. The term "self-help" means just that—it teaches you how to help yourself. There are many books of this kind, geared toward ideas such as: How can I get more of what I desire? What are three steps I can follow to be a millionaire and buy my dream home? What's the secret to getting everything I want in life? These books rarely discuss how to help someone else feel better. What about helping the guy sitting next to you? Or making the cashier feel appreciated? Or complimenting that lady you see every day but never talk to? Or what about simply giving your time, energy, love, money, or lending an ear to someone else?

Have you ever wondered what makes you feel fulfilled? Of course you can feel proud of your achievements and excited about the good news and bright future that await you. We all love winning awards, getting promotions, or getting accepted to our dream school. But that kind of fulfillment is fleeting. How do you really get fulfilled? By doing something for someone else! It's the only surefire way to get that warm, fuzzy, I'm-so-happy-on-the-inside feeling.

Unfortunately, instead of seeking this fulfillment, we go to work every day, sit alone at our computers, and ignore everyone around us unless we need something from them. Get up and go talk to someone! It's called human interaction—it's called being a good human being. And it's healthy!

Today I went on a walk and saw a sixty-two-year-old

neighbor of mine. We started talking, and he explained, "I watched my friend die recently of cancer and it really hit me. I realized that the millions of dollars I've made and all the work I do is self-centered. Everything has been about me. I come off as this nice and friendly guy, but really I'm a pretty selfish person. Eventually, we are all going to have to live with ourselves. If I die without being of use to the people around me, I now realize that I'm going to die unfulfilled. My successful career is going to mean nothing. All it has done is distract me from being a good person, which is probably the purpose of life." I smiled when I heard this last sentence.

You must step outside yourself and your own concerns to discover how much you matter. Fulfillment doesn't come from awards, titles, and paychecks—it comes from being of value to other human beings. And, coincidentally, the more valuable we become to others, the more money, awards, and recognition we receive. It's a paradox—when you work to become more useful to those around you, you get more in return. This is because people are more willing to trust and help someone who helps others. People who become irreplaceably valuable eventually get awarded and promoted for their good work.

When we're trapped inside ourselves and our own needs, wants, and desires, the world is too small to feel free. When we offer ourselves to other people, we step outside the limits of our ego and find that the world is a bit bigger than before. Our identity is pretty limited—it's contained by the thoughts in our heads, the reach of our limbs, and the collection of memories from our experiences. But there's no quantifiable limit your unselfishness can have.

When we reach a plateau in our life in terms of income, happiness, or health, we often think the way to get more is by doing more for ourselves. We often think: Well, I just need to work harder. I just need to treat myself. I just need a vacation. I just need to buy myself this. . . . We look for things to please us and to fulfill us, when, in reality, to find the relief and freedom we crave, we simply need to connect with others. If you want to feel more alive, help someone else feel alive. And if you want to make more money, become more valuable than you've ever been. Shift your focus onto how you can contribute to others, and move it away from all the things you want and need.

Have you ever done a seemingly simple something for someone and realized how good it made you feel? Notice that it's a different feeling from getting the paycheck you've always wanted or being recognized as an award winner. These events give us a sense of pride and excitement, but giving to others fulfills us. It reaches a deeper level of satisfaction that brings us closer to who we are.

In one of his speeches, Simon Sinek—one of my favorite authors—shares an interesting anecdote about an experiment he did with a homeless person. He spoke to a woman who lives on the streets of New York City. She explained that she makes about thirty dollars a day by holding up a sign on a street corner. "The question is," Sinek asks, "how is this person encouraging us to give?" Many homeless people sit with their outdoor advertising that says they're hungry or have kids needing this or that—"Please help me." Their signs explain that you should help them because they were a veteran or they need to feed their children. No matter what it says, it tends to be about them and why you should give them your money. They just talk about themselves. "But the joke," Sinek explains, "is that they act like every corporation today."

Don't most companies operate the same way? They also tend to talk about themselves and why you should buy their products. They want you to know why they are the best, how long they've been around, why they are better than the competition, what deals they have, and why their new product rocks. It's all about them. Sinek adds, "So even if we buy their product, we don't get much feeling out of it."

The homeless woman whom Sinek spoke to normally makes between twenty and thirty dollars a day over a period of ten hours. However, one day she let Sinek change the words on her sign, and she made forty dollars in two hours. Perhaps she would have made more, but after those two hours she left the street corner. In two hours she was able to make more than she normally makes in ten. So what did the sign say to generate such great results? "If you only give once a month, please think of me next time."

Sinek explains that this sign was effective because it didn't discuss the receiver but focused instead on the giver. It didn't focus on the person asking for something; it was about the person giving something. Sinek proposes that it was successful because it addressed the giver's concerns. He adds, "Most people say they can't give to everyone. How do they know the person really needs it? I need it too." So in the sign he addressed both of those concerns: "I know you can't give to everyone. So, if you give only once a month, my desires are authentic and I'll still be here when you're ready to give." This made the money the woman needed about others and not about her. By using this approach, she got what she wanted and helped others get what they want—to feel like they are actually making a difference for someone who really needs their help. This creates a sustainable win-win scenario.

It doesn't matter if it's a coworker, customer, client, or your boss—they are all people and they are all worth helping. When you make things about others, and not about yourself, you'll be astounded by how far you go in business and life. You'll realize that, regardless of someone's perceived importance to you, you limit yourself when your focus is just on your wants and needs.

✳

O̲N̲C̲E̲ ̲U̲P̲O̲N̲ ̲A̲ time there was a man who wanted to be a millionaire. So he did market research and saw what was selling. He found a factory that could make the product three times cheaper than his competitors. It wouldn't be of as high quality, but his production costs would be much lower. The market indicated that this product was in fact selling, so he figured a slight drop in quality would make no difference and he could become rich. He did his calculations and determined the sales he needed to get what he wanted.

When he released the product, he marketed it well, and during the first week it broke sales records. He knew he was on his way to getting rich! Sales were growing, and so he took out an extremely large line of credit to cover a purchase order for more products. He wasn't worried about doing this, because the product would be extremely cheap per piece, and he knew that his profit margin would be massive. He was so excited!

Just as he received the giant shipment, he noticed that sales started to drop. Wondering what was the matter, he went to Amazon.com and saw that his product was receiving awful reviews. "Do not buy this! It's cheaply made and is the same price as the competitors. Buy another brand! This stinks!" Nearly in tears of frustration, he told himself that everything was okay—that he would lower the price and the product would sell again. Months passed and his sales came to a halt.

His brand was now considered a rip-off. People could see that it was all about profit. He was unable to repay his credit, so he sold his home and declared bankruptcy. His stress levels were off the charts.

Years later, the man—helpless, broke, and depressed—bumped into a young, beautiful woman while turning the corner. She dropped everything in her hands when their shoulders collided.

"I'm so sorry!" he said. "I wasn't looking! It's my fault!" He bent down to pick up what she had dropped, and to his surprise he found a product similar to the one he had once sold. All he could do was stare at it. To his amazement, the product had every feature he had elected not to incorporate because his main focus was on low production costs. "Wow! I once had a business selling these! How's yours doing?" he asked.

The woman's smile was almost too bright and beautiful for the man to look at. "How cool!" she said. "It's flying off the shelves. I just can't believe it!"

"Wow! What's your secret?" he asked.

"I wanted to solve every problem I possibly could for the customer! I wanted to change the way our industry does business!" she responded, before carrying on with her day.

That night, after some research, the man learned that this woman was worth twenty million dollars and rising. Her product was considered the best in the industry. Customer reviews raved about how the product had affected their lives and how thankful they were for finding it. The man did not sleep for a week.

IF YOU THINK only about yourself and what you can get, you will find limitations and unmet expectations. To grow rich, you must understand what the world needs and fill that need selflessly. It needs to be about something bigger than you. This is what the woman in the story did. She had other people in mind when she worked. Her business was about solving a problem. By fulfilling others' needs she became rich.

I'm always in awe when I give keynote speeches at business and marketing conferences. Everyone talks about how to engage with customers, drive bottom lines, fine-tune designs, and scale companies. I wish we would add another couple of items to the list, such as: How can we help the human race progress? How can we inspire others to feel more confident and empowered? How can we make a genuine difference in people's lives?

Walt Disney said, "We don't make movies to make money. We make money to make movies." If our work is only about what we get, then we are no more valuable than the next competitor who is out to get theirs. What makes Apple, Apple? What makes Disney, Disney? Skills, resources, and application alone do not define success—success is also about how you view what you're doing. Is your focus solely on personal gain? You can go only so far if that's your primary motive. However, if your focus is on offering something to someone else, you tap into a power greater than yourself—and that power catapults you forward.

This is what I like to call the "catapult effect": being pushed to new heights of success and influence because of your ability to inspire and serve other people.

Apple, Disney, and TOMS shoes have experienced the catapult effect by developing a personal connection with their customers—they have purposes beyond making sales. We don't see them as companies trying to earn money and nothing else. Apple tries to push the barriers in technology, Disney wants to help us dream, and TOMS wants to make the world a place where every child has shoes. Each company has a meaning, purpose, and mission.

Have you ever seen anyone with a Halliburton or a General Electric tattoo or a sticker for those companies on their car or computer? Probably not. How about an Apple sticker? I have, and most likely you have too. These kind of brands offer more than a product, so they are remembered and trusted. They have developed into symbols that not only say something about who they are but also make you feel a part of that something. It feels almost as though they are saying: Hey! We care about you! We want to give you this beautiful thing that will add value to your life! And when we feel appreciated and accepted into the culture of these companies, we are proud to represent them—we feel that it says something about who we are.

Whether you're starting a company, working at a desk at someone else's company, or somewhere in between, you will become more successful by focusing on being more valuable to others. Everything you do sends out a signal about who you are and what you believe in. That's why the man with the product, in the story earlier, found a lot of success at the beginning—he attracted people to his product and company. But after a while, people noticed that his brand was really just about getting their money—it was only self-serving—which made it less valuable to them. This is why people bought products from the woman's company instead—a company that was truly out to make its customers' lives better.

When we act like the man's company, working to get what we want and need, people eventually realize it and say: I'm not sure these people are there for me. I don't know if I can trust them. They seem too focused on themselves. Whether we are acting as organizations or individuals, we should step outside the things we want and offer ourselves to others. Just like Zig Ziglar once said: "If you help enough people get what they want, you will get everything you want."

Show up, at your work and in your life, for something greater than yourself. Your part is to tap into something larger, so other people can be inspired and aided in their lives. The people and brands that have something to offer are the ones we are interested in. We buy their products and identify with them. If they are people, they are the ones we want around us, the ones we eventually end up paying and appreciating more.

Sometimes we don't know why we are attracted to someone's company or want to hire them—what they offer seems inexplicable and intangible. They aren't necessarily the smartest or the most skilled. They may not even be acknowledged every time they are present, but their absence is clearly noticed.

That intangible thing we notice is called "presence." It is their essence. They have stepped outside their egos for the greater good of those around them, which has made them a vital piece of the puzzle.

You know the guy on the basketball team who isn't the best but is always picked? The guy who doesn't score that many points and doesn't load up the box score with statistics? Maybe you don't even notice when he is there, but you need him on your team, and you notice when he's gone.

I am sure many of you who have played team sports know exactly whom I'm talking about. The need for this player is proof that success is not about what you have and get but what you have to offer.

"Where's Suzy today? I miss her energy!" "Where's Bob today? I need to see his smile!" Being missed shows that you make a difference in other people's lives. And isn't that the definition of success? Strive to make it so next time you come back from being away, people say, "Where have you been? It's so good to hear your voice."

Try to have your absence felt—which doesn't necessarily mean your presence is always noticed. You may not be the flashiest, most skilled, loudest, or most decorative person around, but that's not important. What is important is to strive to create value—to be the type of person who is missed when they're not around.

When I was a high school and college basketball player, and often the captain of my team, I would focus on the few people I thought would help me win games—the best knockdown shooters, the tallest players, the ones who averaged a lot of points and made flashy plays. Toward the end of the season, when every game mattered, one of our bench players, who still logged a good amount of minutes per game, was sick. I didn't always notice him. He didn't score much. He wasn't the person I looked for when I was dribbling down the court. He rarely showed up in the box-score statistics; but when he was gone, his absence was felt.

Why aren't we getting the loose balls this game? Where's the gritty defense? Who can guard the big guys? Why aren't we getting the hustle plays? Where are all our rebounds? Where's a hard screen to set the tempo of our toughness? "Oh, yeah," I remembered after the game. "We didn't have Andrew Jury." After that, I never again forgot to acknowledge and appreciate his overlooked, yet essential, energy!

What I learned from Andrew was that if you want to win, do the things it takes to win—even if they are un-glamorous. If you want to get what you want, do the things no one else is willing to do. Give the stuff no one else is willing to give. In today's world, that often means being of value rather than merely aiming for success. Be the person whose energy is missed when you're not around. People who create good numbers in sales or basketball shots are often replaceable—someone else can be trained to do that. But valuable energy is hard to teach or replace. It's developed through the will to be the kind of person no one else is committed to becoming. It begins and ends with an open heart.

Your energy might be categorized as one of two things: infectious or infecting. In each situation you encounter, for every person you pass in the hallway, every conversation you have, whenever you walk into a room, your energy will be *infectious*, a palpable surge of positivity, or an *infecting* sludge of dust. You are either lifting people up or you are not. You may not be putting people down, but you are certainly not infectious if you are not making an effort to light a spark in the eyes of those you come in contact with.

We've all heard the story of the underdog in sports or business who makes it. But how did they do it? They didn't go to an Ivy League school—in fact, they didn't go to college at all. They were not qualified. They didn't have the resources or the test scores. Their parents didn't help them out. So how did they do it? "I don't know," we say. "They just have it."

What's "it"? It is a presence. It's something that emanates from your being and intoxicates others. It's your essence. It's this thing about you that makes other people feel good. It makes other people around you feel comfortable, safe, inspired, motivated, and generous. It's your vibe. Unlike most people's, your energy is not confined to your personal concerns. Your energy isn't wasted on the trivial things that constrict most of us—all our wants, needs, to-dos, desires, and concerns. You are just different—your presence is felt.

You have *it* when you step outside yourself. You become a bigger person than you ever thought possible. You may not have all the skills that others do, but you manage to get things done and to help others do the same. It's the way you interact, talk, and carry yourself. It's the way you treat others. You have a presence that emanates from you—it goes beyond who you are as a person. Philosophers in ancient Greece, like Plato, had huge discussions about this presence, which they ended up calling "the Good." It's the spirit of who you are—it's what people feel about you.

Check in with yourself each day; every time you step into the office or your home ask yourself: How can I embody the Good? How can I spark joy?

When we meet someone with this presence we often say, "That person has such good energy." That's because they've stepped outside themselves. Their energy is no longer confined within the limits of "me." It's expansive and has an impact on other people. It's something that is felt but not always measurable. That's why it's so hard for us to describe what constitutes a great leader. The essence of a leader is an intangible element, but one that sweeps up everything in its path to create something good.

People will remember only how you make them feel. In your pursuit of a better future for yourself, do not neglect the most important thing of all—other people. You'll likely make a lot of money if you become more valuable. You'll likely get the car, the house, the awards, and whatever else you want. But if your aim is to be truly happy, and not just cluttered with a bunch of expensive and pretty distractions that flatter your ego and cover up a meaningless life, you mustn't forget to care and to offer your love.

If one of your aims is to go far in life and achieve great success (which it certainly doesn't have to be), remember to be of value as a human being, not just as a worker. Don't give only stuff that you can buy, have, or own. Give yourself. Give your attention. Be someone whose presence is missed when you are out of the office; be someone who creates so much good for others that they notice and miss you when you're not around.

This is what I'd been telling a friend of mine who was depressed. But he just couldn't grasp what I was saying. Finally, one day he got it. He said, "I know how to get myself out of this depression!" He then went on to tell me how he and his girlfriend walked into the 24 Hour Fitness they always go to, and the guy behind the desk said, "You're the coolest people here—the nicest couple. You always stop and talk to me like you have nowhere else to be. You are just chill, and it feels good." Hearing that made my friend feel extremely happy. He forgot about his depression and stress. He was totally connected to something larger than himself and his problems.

We all want to feel significant and happy. I believe that the image we have of ourselves is what determines how we feel. Sometimes we have little images of ourselves: we feel insignificant, and so we feel depressed—as if no one notices us or we don't matter. We get stuck inside ourselves, feel trapped within our lives.

Human beings need to feel significant to feel happy. The question is, how do we find significance? Some of the ways we seek significance and fulfillment trap us within ourselves—trying to be number one; aiming solely to get the next raise; climbing the ladder for the next title; bragging about our achievements; telling dramatic stories for reactions; complaining about problems so people give us attention; becoming workaholic; spending a lot of money on fashionable clothing so that people stop, look, and compliment us; becoming the most successful person we know. All these things trap us within ourselves. They perpetuate a never-ending cycle of needing and wanting more things. It's not that these things are bad or unhealthy, but they are all about me, me, me. They provide only fleeting feelings of contentment, so we constantly need more of them to reaffirm our significance and identity.

To really come alive as a human being, you have to stop being trapped in yourself, your concerns, and your desires, and start showing up for other people. The time has come for us to realize that this isn't some childish concept. We hear it from some of the world's most successful people. Remember what Justine Musk said when asked how her husband, Elon Musk, had become one of the most powerful businessmen in the world: "Shift your focus away from what you want and get deeply, intensely curious about what the world wants and needs. It helps to have an ego, but you must be in service to something bigger."

Anyone who wants more fulfillment or success needs to be aware of what makes them feel significant. My friend who was depressed found it a great accomplishment when the guy working at the gym acknowledged him and his girlfriend as his favorite people there, in a place brimming with countless bodies every day. It gave him a sense of significance; it showed him that even in this overcrowded world, he matters to someone. It showed him how much bigger he and the world become when he steps outside himself and offers his presence wholeheartedly to others.

Being successful isn't about working hardest, being smartest, or making the most sales. It's about being full of love and letting your actions define you. It's not about what you say. It's about what you do and how you respond when things do not go as you desired.

Your identity is not defined by the books you read or where you graduated from college—it's defined by the number of times you keep your cool and help others, even when it would be easier to give up. Being a valuable human being is about showing up every day and knowing that at the end of the day all that matters is that you stepped outside your ego and were fully present for the people around you. In a world where almost everyone is focused on themselves, someone who is a constant light for others is a rare commodity.

Albert Einstein once said that the true value of a human being can be found in the degree to which they have attained liberation from the self. And Martin Luther King Jr. said that to be free we must step outside the narrow confines of our personal concerns and look to the broader ones of those around us. We find life more pleasant and are more productive when we get outside our heads.

I have to do this. Now that I've completed that, I'll go there. Did I remember to pay the rent? I wonder if I have any new text messages? What will I have for dinner? What will I wear tomorrow? How do I look? Is my hair okay? I wonder if these shoes look good? Are they even noticing me? The movie last night was great. I can't believe the news! Last week was wonderful! Is there anything I should be doing?

Does this sound familiar? We've spent many years of our lives trying to figure out what we want and what we need to do, and it has gotten us this far. But maybe the new question to ask ourselves is, *where would I be if I figured out how to make others feel more joy and inspiration?* Take some time to think and write about this. You may be surprised by what you discover.

Significance that lasts and deeply fulfills you comes from being a positive light, especially in seemingly mundane situations. This means that we are not free until we step outside the narrow confines of ourselves. Be a light for someone else and you will find light in your life. We can trick ourselves into believing that to feel happiness, significance, and to make a difference we must write a book, start a business, or make a million dollars. We can trick ourselves into thinking that pleasing ourselves with temporarily satisfying things will keep us going, but as long as we are stuck in the search to create our identity through achievement, we cannot really be free. In fact, it is quite the opposite that will bring us freedom. The beauty in attempting to be a light for another, which is the process of stepping outside yourself, is that you lose self-consciousness. Your problems do not exist. Nothing exists other than the moment taking place—a moment where you are a willing instrument directing your love toward others.

This loss of identity, this freedom from oneself, this beautiful sense of significance and value comes from how the people at work or in the hallways, elevators, gyms, stores, your home, and your street feel about you—it's about how you make them feel. Have you left an impression that momentarily lightened the weight of the day, or are you just another face too busy to offer your love?

Now imagine how much your worth would increase over a twelve-month span at work, home, or school if you became that type of person to everyone around you. You would become irreplaceable. At work you would become more significant. At home your roommates, family, or lover(s) would appreciate you more deeply. At school your colleagues, classmates, and teachers would recognize the warm environment you're creating.

Too often we simply tell the person behind the cash register what we want and move on, or we just say hi to our coworker and nothing more. We aren't rude, but we aren't warm either. Acting this way doesn't allow us to be valuable to our immediate environment. It's in the little things, like everyday interactions with people, that we find our significance and increase our worth.

If we accept this truth, how can life be void of meaning? How could you not increase your accolades and income? How could you possibly feel depressed? How could you feel insignificant if you made someone smile who seemed down? How could you feel like you don't matter if someone's face becomes brighter and more beautiful because of your presence? How could you feel insignificant if the people at the places you constantly go to start to remember you, notice you, smile at you, and seem happy to see you again?

That's significance. That's stepping outside yourself for the greater good of those around you. That's how you build a larger, more powerful self-image. That's how you find out how much you matter.

Try it out. Tell yourself that your one goal is to have meaningful connections with the people who work at the places you consistently go to, and see if they will open up to you. See if you can momentarily lift the weight of the day off their shoulders. See how that positively affects their interactions with others and how much more productive and at ease they are while working after you do.

Step outside yourself. *Be the one who makes people feel like they matter, and you will find out how much you matter.* Just yesterday, my girlfriend said, "I looked in the mirror at myself earlier, and I am the prettiest I've ever looked and felt in my entire life. I'm telling you because a lot of the way I feel comes from the way you talk to me all the time." While I can't take that much credit, I can tell you how happy that made me. I believe that you and I as human beings have been given an *incredible* honor: with our words and energy we can help build the image people have of themselves into something beyond anything they've ever experienced. If that isn't something to *take pride* in, I don't know what is.

Last week I gave a speech at a high school. While there, I learned that a girl had just committed suicide because of how people treated her. Hers was a death that could have been prevented by people like you and me. Just a *few* loving words could've changed everything. If only someone had stepped up . . .

People's minds are like clay that can be imprinted with the things you do and the words you speak. Take great pride in the way those around you view themselves—it is a reflection of who you are. How big or small the people around you feel is often a reflection of how big or small you act.

People often become the spitting image of the way they are treated by those around them. If you sense that someone's self-esteem or self-image is low, or you just want to step up your game, ask yourself this: Who am I being? How can I be bigger? What can I do to build people up? Let's take serious pride in this task.

For too long we've determined value through material measures—numbers, houses, cars, buildings. But what determines the value of these inanimate objects? People do. People have real value, and their ability to give is of real substance. Somehow, however, we've convinced ourselves that we can trade our value to obtain worldly values. If we're selfish long enough, we believe, we'll be able to take care of ourselves.

This type of thinking creates the backward, inside-out, superficial, and corrupted part of society today. We think we need the money, a house, a car, a job, an award, a lover, etc. The "this and that" and "me, me, me." But, in thinking this way, we give away our time, health, sanity, compassion, and connections. We give it all away so we can have what we think we want. And what do we end up with? Objects that do not love us back. Toys—yes, shiny ones, but nevertheless toys that won't last. Full-size versions of the Lincoln Logs houses we built as kids—our dream homes that we slaved away to buy and that we continue to maintain at the expense of our connection to those around us.

What would aliens think of our society? I think they either have already found our civilization and thought: "Wow! These people are so barbaric, so backward. They clobber each other, blow each other up, climb to the top of glass buildings hoping to be number one, and compete against each other to find significance instead of stopping and taking care of one another. Wow! We should probably just let them be, and keep ourselves safe." They probably see us as disconnected from what life is about and what love is, so they figure there's no use and they should just keep cruising through the galaxy until they find some other beings who have a better appreciation of the cosmic picture. Either that, or aliens don't exist at all.

Either way, it's fun to think about and brings up the question, are we alone? No, actually, we are not alone. Often we feel alone—we feel stuck in a cubicle, in the Rubik's Cube of the nine-to-five, occasionally taking breaks from the choking ordinariness of life by watching our favorite TV shows and searching for the best vacations, when, in reality, we are so scared that we can't even admit we're lost. So we go in endless pursuit of the nicest body, the newest car, the freshest shoes, and the hottest lover anyone has ever seen. And we do this while everyone else runs around so fast that no one has time to wonder if people like us, who have everything, are happy. I mean, we've got all the best gadgetry—we've got to be happy! Right? All I need to do is keep my head down and work harder, and maybe, if I'm lucky, I'll get there one day.

Our lives are in disarray, and the world is in chaos because we're chasing the wrong values. We've been duped. We've been told we need those valuable things to live the good life. Meanwhile, a bunch of people behind the curtains roll wheelbarrows of cash, trying not to laugh too loud because they can hardly believe that we are buying into their game—that we believe we need all these things to be happy.

A common example is the young woman who slaves away for money, only to spend it on a boob job that attracts men who are interested in her only because of her body. She ends up marrying one of these men. Eventually they get divorced. Then she's older and single and decides to use her hard-earned money to look younger, so she gets a face-lift and Botox galore. Later she finds another guy, and the cycle repeats itself until she's very old and cannot compete with time and nature. She wonders why she did all this to her face. Now her breast implants just get in the way of hugging her grandchildren.

Another example is the tired old man who was once a confused young man searching for love. He decided he wanted to be a billionaire business tycoon and put the search for love on hold. "Time to be a man!" he thought. He started working his way up the ladder to success. He made sure his bosses noticed that he was better than everyone else. He made sure he was considered number one at his company. Then the paychecks started building up into more money than he knew what to do with. He was tired and his body ached, but his smile (from all his expensive dental work) looked so good. He kept smiling his pearly whites and kept climbing. "Next stop after the penthouse is the presidential suite!" He went from floor one, at a low-level apartment, to a penthouse, and then to presidential living, with the added bonus of tinted windows on his brand-new sports car.

His body was tight from all the time at his desk, so when he could, he would hit the gym and throw some weights around. He'd pick up the heaviest weights he could and get a good pump in at the gym. He'd look in the mirror and notice his body becoming more desirable—it was big and looked strong. Young women often noticed this seemingly successful man. He drove a nice car, wore expensive clothes, had a shiny new watch, and was often able to take women back to his apartment, which, by the way, had a great view. However, none of those women stayed in his life for very long. Busy reaching every goal, making more money than he could spend, and giving advice to young men, he had forgotten about his initial goal of finding love. He never married and grew old alone.

Eventually his back started going out. He went to the doctor and found it was a tumor in his spine—perhaps caused by all the stress he endured in his work life while he was busy climbing to the top. Six months later he was paralyzed from the neck down, and many years later he died.

Old age and death will make a mockery of us all. Let's not make a mockery of ourselves in the meantime. Let's not be so concerned with ourselves that we lose track of what's most important in life—being of service. Remember what Gandhi said: "The best way to find yourself is to lose yourself in the service of others."

Years ago, I needed some starter capital to fund a speaking tour. At the time, I did not have any funds available. For years, all I'd done on social media was give myself to those who were engaged with my different pages. I answered basically every personal question and sometimes neglected more seemingly important things so that I could help strangers through difficult situations. Every day I posted the best and most heartfelt writings I possibly could.

Therefore when it came time to launch a crowdfunding campaign for my tour, I not only received my intended financial goal but much more. People gave me way more than I could've possibly imagined. Everything clicked—it was the start I needed to do what I do now, which is tour around North America giving inspirational speeches year-round. If you wholeheartedly give and help the people around you, it will come back to you in more surprising ways than you can imagine.

EXERCISES FOR

CREED THREE

- For the rest of the week, make it your intention to step outside yourself. Instead of focusing on everything you need to do for yourself, ask, what can I do for others?
- Check in with yourself each day; every time you step into the office or your home, ask yourself: How can I embody the Good? How can I spark joy? Mark your success according to your ability to be the Good for others and based on how much joy you spark in others.
- Compliment people. Ask them if they need help. Instead of telling yourself you're too busy for a conversation, take two extra minutes to start a conversation and ask questions. Be the joy others need this week.

CREED FOUR

Lend an Ear

LISTENING TO OTHERS is one of the most important skills we can acquire in this lifetime. I do not mean listening just so we know how to respond, but truly listening so the person speaking feels heard and understood. Listening is a selfless act—you have to momentarily let go of what you want so you can help someone else get what they want. When people speak, they usually want to be heard and understood. People feel empowered when others listen to them. By being a good listener you earn respect, become highly valued, and are seen as a leader. Others will know they can count on you.

"That's cool and all, but what does this have to do with making money?" someone may ask. Well, actually, this has a lot to do with making money. In a world of instant connectivity and many possibilities, too many people feel overwhelmed and alone because we don't listen to one another very well, sometimes not at all.

People who learn to listen can more easily establish themselves as leaders—they can build a kind of trust that can only be earned. The more you're trusted—the more you allow others to feel understood—the better leader you will become and the more money you will make.

I spoke with Marian Wright Edelman, one of Martin Luther King Jr.'s close friends and lawyers, and I was shocked when she told me Dr. King inspired people to trust in his vision by listening. "Really? It wasn't his speaking abilities?" I asked, one winter afternoon in Washington, DC. "Absolutely," she said. "But he also had a willingness to lend his ear and listen to other people for hours. People felt truly heard, which made them feel powerful. They trusted him. He learned how to lead by listening and learning how others felt." I almost couldn't believe that someone so close to Martin Luther King Jr., one of the greatest leaders who ever lived, was saying that he empowered people by listening to them.

This is a competitive world. Many of us want to be leaders. We want to be valuable. Thousands of books offer insights about what might help us achieve success. We pay big money for seminars to learn these secrets. Companies budget for motivational speakers and management gurus to teach them how to lead better. Many academics and other writers comment on the qualities of successful people, trying to understand what led to their achievements. During interviews, some tycoons and leaders even demonstrate that they don't know the key to their own success—they adopt clichés and appear less than introspective about themselves. Could it be that we've missed the mark when it comes to what effective leadership entails? Have we overlooked how to truly empower others and how to inspire groups of people toward a common objective?

It's romantic to think that a powerful presence is a matter of how you look and how you project your voice and that image. It's glamorous to think that a leader is the most intelligent or charismatic person in the room. It's hopeful to believe that success is equated with doglike persistence and the tenacity to go after anything you want until you achieve it. But history shows us that Martin Luther King Jr. became one of the most powerful and impactful human beings to walk the face of the earth by being a great listener.

We've developed a culture that is too selfish and has too short an attention span for people to bother to look others in the eyes, listen, and connect. People in workplaces, stores, sidewalks—in fact, just about anyplace you go in the twenty-first century—have lost the ability to listen with the intention of hearing. We listen to respond. We may be silent, so it seems like we're listening, but we're actually thinking about what to say in response, or something totally unrelated, or about how we can graciously end the conversation as quickly as possible.

Have you ever noticed how much joy it sparks when you stop at the cash register or in the hallway long enough to have a genuine interaction with someone passing by? It's awesome. You usually walk away feeling happy. And the other person walks away feeling happy too. By doing something as simple as setting the intention of becoming a more conscious listener, you begin to spark joy in nearly every experience.

I'm often amazed when I get the tour of corporate offices before I am hired to speak. The executives complain about lack of leadership, inspiration, and teamwork. "Do you have any suggestions?" they often ask. "Yes, a good first step would be to get everyone to stop walking with their heads down, and get them to actually look and listen to each other. Maybe the pillars of your business shouldn't be efficiency and productivity but listening and caring. Maybe then people would feel valued and empowered. Maybe then people would be inspired to work with others," I reply.

At the beginning of the book I explained that the MVPs are often a company's worst leaders. They are very skilled at their work but very poor at connecting with others. They are only focused on their personal tasks, the things they need to do. That's why they are so productive, but that's also why so many people complain about their management, communication, and leadership.

We see a similar problem in marriages: they often don't function properly when one partner devotes all his or her time to work. Sometimes one partner, or both, becomes too self-absorbed to ask the other how their day was or to listen to their joys and concerns. If a partner makes not listening a habit, it often leads to divorce.

The same is true in friendship or with colleagues in workplace relationships. Those who make the effort to listen and connect find that people not only trust them more but are also inspired by them. They begin to want to help and show up every day because they feel valued. They know that if they have something to say, they will be heard. We value leaders who listen because it's much easier for us to respect someone who makes us feel understood.

Think about it. If someone on the street—someone you don't know—asks you for a favor, you will probably tell him to leave you alone. If an acquaintance wants your time or help, you might hesitate, wondering what he has done for you, if you trust him, or if you feel respected by him. You might end up helping him even if you don't feel heard and respected. And even if you don't trust him, you still might perform the favor, but halfheartedly. You won't be invested in it. And if you do feel invested, it might be because you feel obligated to be a good person. However, when someone you really respect and trust comes to you, someone whom you know listens to you, appreciates your feedback, and genuinely cares about you as a human being—when that person asks for a favor, things are different. You want to help her and make her happy. You are much more likely to help champion her vision. You are much more willing to serve and take risks. You are motivated to do good work. You want to say yes. Why? Because you trust her. She cares about you, and you know that she will listen to you if you have a concern. You know she will not neglect you. You are confident she will be there for you if and when you need an ear or a hand.

President Woodrow Wilson once said, "The ear of a leader must ring with the voices of the people." I couldn't agree more. Anyone, regardless of their title in the workplace or the world, can become a leader by applying this simple principle. People are inspired and motivated by those who make them feel like their voice matters. We don't need to acquire new skills or to get a promotion to become a great leader. We need to reestablish the lost art of selfless listening—we must make sure people are heard once again.

In the name of progress, too many people have been silenced, their feelings forgotten, and their concerns washed over. This leads to loss of motivation and, in worst-case scenarios, loss of a job. "I don't know what Bob's deal is. He's not very engaged anymore. He's pretty checked out." Why don't you ask him how he's feeling and listen to what he says? But we hardly ever do ask and listen.

It's a simple concept that we often overlook. We want complexity. We look for big, romantic ideals to lead our lives. We don't realize that everything would change in work and life if we kept it simple and lent our ears more wholeheartedly.

We must start a shift in culture. We must start listening to one another. Gandhi's words, "be the change you wish to see in the world," are even applicable to how we might add more value to the marketplace. You should take a look at what the workplace, economy, and people of the world need, and then begin to do that, especially if no one else is. This is listening. The more you listen, the more you empower others, and you also empower yourself by becoming more valuable to others. Having real value to offer those around you is a sure step not only toward fulfillment but toward making money as well.

Many of us are too often in a frenzy of fidgety craziness, as if we were overcaffeinated tweakers convinced that we must keep pace and move on to the next thing. The next what? The next paper? So you can do another? The next meeting?

Have you ever been one minute late for something, racing to get there, stampeding along in a sweat, only to find that when you walk into the room, playing it cool as though you weren't really stressing, that it's actually starting ten minutes later? And then, suddenly, maybe you feel kind of worthless because you didn't take time to talk to Betty about her son's basketball season. Maybe you, like me, used to play basketball, and that conversation would have made you smile, thinking about when you were a kid. And if you did, you would have been a whole seventy-four seconds late, with the excuse of being a good person who connects with others. I would rather be an always-late-and-in-a-very-good-vibe kind of person than an on-the-dot tight-butt or an I'm-too-busy-for-life kind of wretch. Ideally, we should be able to be on time and be totally connected to everyone (but let's move forward in baby steps).

Meanwhile, businesses blunder and economies amass debt because most people in companies and on city side-walks have forgotten about one another. Maybe it's really this simple: if your company is losing money, people are quitting, and you've tried training after training to improve your managers, maybe you don't need any more business training. Maybe you just need to listen—to let people feel heard, seen, loved, and acknowledged.

When people feel heard, they begin to hear and trust the vision within themselves. They become more self-assured and confident. They are more pleasant to be around and eventually become leaders themselves.

It feels like a miracle has occurred when you eventually notice that for the past thirty-three seconds all your troubles have dissolved because you've been listening to someone with all your self and senses. You literally forgot about yourself. You become so enmeshed in your experience that your identity nearly dissolves into a space of love where another person can be heard. That's what happens when you really listen.

The personal freedom you and I both crave is to be found outside the narrow confines of ourselves. When we're no longer trapped in our identities, stories, and problems, we're free. And one way to step outside of that confinement is by listening—by letting ourselves dissolve into love for another, perhaps even for a stranger.

The day we do this is the day we will see the suicide rate drop, job happiness increase, fulfillment at home skyrocket, and productivity loss turn into rising profits. All this will happen because people will feel like they are seen for who they are and are thus happy to put forth their best for others.

Recently, I spoke at a public high school in San Diego. Afterward, one of the students asked if she could record me for a tribute video she was making for one of the students, Taylor, who had committed suicide a few days before. Taylor took her life because she felt no one cared about her and that she didn't matter. Since then I've shared her story at every single school I've spoken at. After each speech, stories pile in from students who have had someone lend an ear or care for them in a time of need, stories about how it changed their life.

Why is it that we live in a world brimming with people but we feel so alone? I stare through my window, at the gray clouds, and hear a couple argue. "What's wrong? Is everything okay?" one says. "You never listen to me!" the other shrieks. "I do listen!" the first one answers, as quickly as possible.

But are we really listening?

Have you ever felt that overbearing sense of frustration when you are trying to explain something and the person you're speaking to keeps moving their mouth as if to interrupt? What are the chances you do that to other people? Sometimes I notice the tension in my body grow while someone is speaking to me—especially when I want to get on with my day or to respond. Their words become a murmur hidden behind the thoughts in my head. "I'm busy. I need to get going. How long are they going to keep blabbing?" I look at them like they're an egomaniac who wants to steal my time. Then, when they walk away and carry on with their day, I land back in reality. I realize that listening to their few words required so little time, perhaps thirty bats of my eyelashes, yet I was so trapped in the matrix of myself that I was convinced I'd miss opportunities, that life was passing me by, if I didn't figure out how to end the conversation soon. "Well, I've got to get going." Or, "It was great to see you, but pardon me, please, I have to hop on the phone now. Have a great day!"

Sometimes I've even pretended to be on my cell phone so I don't have to talk to my neighbor. He's older than I am, sixty-two. He is lonely. Our conversations, even when I do just listen, never last more than five minutes. When I really don't want to talk, they end up being fifteen, maybe thirty seconds. I imagine he goes back to his apartment and sits there. I often hear classical piano music coming from his window when I walk by. I can see the loneliness in his eyes—then I wonder if I am really seeing my own eyes? What kind of a person am I if I convince myself that interactions aren't worth having unless I am the one speaking? Who does that make me? Is this how my mother raised me? Is that how your mother raised you?

When we're little we're told to do a few things with our time, but the main thing we're told is to be kind and to care for others. Have you ever talked with a child—not in passing, but just the two of you on a couch or someplace? Kids really want to know things and ask tons of cute questions. You respond, and they listen. You spark their curiosity like a shooting star burning in the sky. Their minds jump to another question. They ask. You answer. They listen. And it goes on and on: Wow! What do you mean? It's like that? Really? How come? Are you sure? Why is that? What else? Kids just want to know.

It feels so good when someone genuinely wants to know something about you. Have you ever had someone listen to you—just listen to you—so magnificently? It's one of the best gifts in the world! But we grow up and have things to say, places to be, stuff to check off our lists, thoughts to think, and priorities to bear in mind. We forget to listen.

We see it in the movies. You, the adult, are a bit overwhelmed with everything. You're walking in the park. You don't feel the wind on your face, nor do you see the leaves fall in front of you. You hardly feel your feet touching the soft grass. The sounds of children playing around you go almost unnoticed. You're thinking. You take a seat, wondering what to do. You're at a crossroads and you can't decide. You want to pour these thoughts from your head like a morning cup of orange juice—get them out of your head so you can feel again. Feel freedom. Feel happiness. Feel. No longer be trapped inside your noggin.

Then—*bam!* Everything spins for a second as you see only pink. You fall backward from your seat, onto the ground. You swing at whatever just hit you—you don't know what it is. For all you know, you're being attacked by terrorists! You lie on your back and take a shallow breath. It's interrupted by a high-pitched innocent voice, "I'm sorry! It's windy!" You open your eyes: a hired assassin has not attacked you because you are late paying your bills, it's just a little girl, about seven years old, standing there. Joy oozes through her missing front teeth like the wind whistling on chimes. A blonde with pigtails and pink hair ties stands before you. You sit up and realize it was her small kite that hit you. You're a little embarrassed by the way you jumped for your life and had no idea what happened. You hand the girl her kite and tell her it's okay. You smirk, but it's half-assed, like part of you wants to smile but the other part of your brain never heard the message because it's still thinking about bills, work, and relationships.

"Having fun?" you ask her.

"Yes. What are you doing?" she says.

"I'm just thinking. Trying to figure something out. I had a long week," you say to her, like she just wouldn't understand.

"What happened?" she asks. Her question makes your mind turn a million miles per second. You think about everything. Your future. Your past. Your troubles. All the things you imagine she just wouldn't understand.

"Just grown-up stuff. It's not that big of a deal," you say.

"Like what?" she asks.

"Well . . ." You tell her that your boss is kind of mean and you never know whether you're going to get fired. You're under a lot of stress to complete projects on time, but you owe money on your credit card and it's hard to focus and be productive when you're short on cash and probably will be for the long term. There's also the issue of the lack of a fulfilling romantic relationship. And there's anxiety about the future. There's what you wish or should've done . . . Not to mention that you still don't know why you're not getting a response from you-know-who about you-know-what. "So, you see, it's been a long day." You sigh.

"I see," the little girl says. "Do you have a home and money for dinner?" You laugh and nod your head.

"Because if you don't, I can ask my mom if you can have dinner with us and stay at our house. She's over there." You look to where the little girl points, and a beautiful woman with brown hair tossed by the wind waves and walks your way.

"Hi there! I am so sorry if she's bothering you. Come on, darling, let's head home for supper."

You smile a huge smile. "No! She wasn't bothering me at all. She was just listening to me tell her about the troubles of growing up. I had a long day, but now I feel much better, thanks to her! It looks like your daughter is well on her way to becoming a therapist!"

You all giggle.

"It looks like you have a new friend," the mother says as she looks at her daughter, who is staring at you. You smile.

"I asked him to dinner," the little girl says.

"Well, do you want to come? I've got soup ready. We're

the house just on the corner there!" the mother asks. You decline, with gratitude.

They pick up their things, and the little girl asks, "What are you going to do now?" You tell her you're going to make some supper, send a few e-mails, and get everything sorted out so you can enjoy the weekend.

"Well . . . what are you doing this weekend?" She responds with another question.

"Um . . . I guess I'll just relax and enjoy it. Maybe watch a couple of movies."

"Oh man, that sounds like fun! See you later!" the little girl says, as she grabs her mother's hand and they turn and walk away. "Can we watch a movie too?" you hear her say to her mother, as they fade out in the distance.

You sigh deeper than your usual small, suffocating breaths allow you to. You breathe in through your nose for a good five or six seconds, then you hold your breath and feel the air in your lungs before you slowly let it go. You stand up and head home.

With your hands on the steering wheel, you smile and laugh at how you jumped like a baby when the pink kite hit you, and at how precious little children are. It makes you think about when you were a kid—the memories bring your mind to a wonderful place. You're happy.

It makes you think of your parents. You call them, on the hands-free speaker, just to say hi. "What's up?

Everything okay?" both of them ask. Clearly they were not expecting you to call and have nothing to say other than "I was just thinking about you."

"Yeah . . . everything is great!" You laugh. "Can't I just call you to see what you're up to?" You can't see this through the phone, but they both have huge smiles on their faces. They were just sitting around, thinking about life, fiddling with this, tinkering with that. They were also wondering how you were doing and dreaming about when you were young.

"Oh, well . . ." Your parents sound pleasantly surprised that you've called with nothing to tell or ask them. Ten or fifteen minutes pass. "Hello? You still there?" your mother stops and asks with bewilderment.

"Hello! Yes. What do you mean? I'm here! Can you hear me?" you toss back.

"Oh, okay, great! It just sounded quiet, and I was talking for a minute so I didn't know if I lost you in bad service."

"I was just listening to you," you say.

"Well, thank you! And thanks for calling. I love you! I'll let you get going now. You probably don't want to listen to me blabber about being old all Friday night."

"No!" you say. "This made my Friday night!" You exchange good-byes and hang up.

Your parents are getting older and sometimes they feel lonely. They will call you in a week if you don't call sooner.

They will tell you about how nice it was that you called and listened.

You go to sleep that night with a peace of mind you haven't felt in a long time. No tossing or turning in the sheets. "Wow! I slept great!" you say to yourself when you wake up in the morning.

You reflect on yesterday and realize that everything was out of the norm. A little girl lent you her ear, listening to you so cutely for only, like, three minutes, but it completely changed your day. For the first time in a few months you felt all the weight lift off your shoulders.

Your parents slept wonderfully too. They were so happy that you called. Their worries weren't there after your call.

Well, what happened? Was it magic? No. These are the results of active listening. *Active* listening is listening to understand, listening to hear. *Reactive* listening is hearing what someone says so you can respond and say what you want to say. Reactive listening is there's-somewhere-I-have-to-be or something-I-have-to-say-so-I'm-not-really-listening listening.

The philosopher Diogenes said, "We have two ears and one tongue so that we would listen more and talk less." That's why we should never pretend to know people until we listen to them. We should never be in too much of a hurry to connect with others. We should be aware of our choices and listen consciously.

Have you ever heard the adage "Big egos have little ears"? People notice when we are too caught up in ourselves to care for others. People notice and they stop trusting us. They know they can't really count on us.

You can become a real leader only when you've developed the skill of active listening—when you know how to lend your ear to understand and empower others. Just listen. It will affect your life and the lives of those around you.

CREED FOUR

■ Go out and start a conversation, only to listen. Ask questions and work for a minute or two to reverse the conversation so it focuses on the person you're talking to. Practice listening. Notice how your body feels. Get your awareness out of your head and the millions of thoughts that want to chime into the conversation. Instead, just be present. Be an active listener. After thirty seconds, stop the person and repeat something they said. For example, "So you're saying . . ." It's amazing how others' perceptions of you can skyrocket when they feel like you listen.

Don't Take Anything Personally

Now that you know the difference between active and reactive listening, you are ready to be aware of how you interpret messages. When hearing others, we must try to trust our initial instincts and not add fears and mind games to what was said. For example, if you are told that someone has wronged you, that your work or idea has been rejected, or that someone has said something tasteless about you, remember exactly what you heard. Remember that they *didn't* say any of this happened to purposely hurt you.

"My boss isn't being kind." Leave it at that. "They told me no." Okay. "They are always rude to me." Walk around them. "People are always saying I'm not good enough." Let them talk. Don't feel compelled to add "Why are these things happening to me? Why don't they get it?"

You cannot be responsible for the actions or reactions of others. You are responsible only for you. What matters is what *you* think of you. We live in a world of subjective perceptions. Everyone has his or her own point of view, which is what adds color and diversity to the world. But among all these opinions and all this noise, your view of you is what's important. It's the only view you will ever experience the world from. Anyone who judges, rejects, or condemns you is simply expressing their point of view. It has nothing to do with you. You can keep your happiness and move on with your day.

When you truly understand that it's not about you, and is actually about them, you can let other people's bad energy soar past you like clouds in the sky. What the clouds are doing does not have to affect what you do. If clouds move in a certain way, you don't take it personally and say, "The clouds are doing that thing again—that thing I don't like!" It would be a unique way to see the world, but you probably don't see it that way.

You can treat other people's opinions just like clouds. They are objects outside you. You don't have to feel insulted or upset when people do something that offends you. When the clouds move a certain way, it is not a reflection of you and has no connection to your peace. What someone says or does is not a reflection of you and does not have to affect your peace either.

The viewpoint of someone who does not take things personally looks like this: I live my life; I do not live your life. I am the words I speak, not the words you speak about me. I am the things I do, not the things that happen to me.

Author Don Miguel Ruiz says, "Taking everything personally is the ultimate expression of selfishness—because we are making the assumption that everything is about *me*." In reality, what someone says or does is actually about them—not about you.

You may think: How can I not take things personally when my parent (or ex-lover or coworker or boss or customer) walks in the door unhappy and rude. No matter what I do, with as much compassion as I feel, it doesn't make a difference! But the truth is, we do not know what people are going through. We do have the right to be kind and let people know what we believe, to stand up for our truth, and to have our own opinions. And we have the power not to be affected by everything people say and do. We are responsible only for what we say and do. We aren't even responsible for how others react to us.

If you do your best to spark joy in them but all that comes back from them is negativity, do not take it personally. You do not know what someone is going through.

Keep smiling. You cannot force anyone to change into anything, even if you really wish that they would, even if you're doing your best to be positive and make them feel loved. We do not have the right to try to control people, to force them to behave as we like. Everyone will come around with time. We need to understand this. When we realize that this is the way reality works, we can find peace within ourselves and with everyone else.

Your body is a molecular structure. It's a mass of energy that vibrates at a very high speed. We have invented a word to describe this vibration—we call it "feeling." You ask someone how they are doing, and they will say: "I'm feeling great." "I'm feeling good." "I'm feeling fine." "I'm feeling okay." You'll rarely hear anyone say, "I'm consciously aware of being emotionally involved with a negative idea and therefore have moved into a negative vibration." But, in reality, that's exactly what happens. When you are aware that someone's opinion or action is causing you to feel bad, that's good: because you can change it. You don't have to take it personally. It doesn't have to affect you any more than it already has. You can be in control of your feelings.

Often we let other people upset us, but we don't have to. We can listen to what they are saying and, instead of reacting, we can simply respond. We can say, "Well, you're entitled to your opinion, but that's just not how I am." In this way, we separate their opinion about us and allow ourselves to hold our own ideas about ourselves.

We have this beautiful thing called the "conscious mind." The conscious mind is just that: our consciousness. Now, you may not be the boss at your workplace, but you are the boss of your mind. Your conscious mind creates how you feel in the moment. If you panic, thoughts of panic send an electric signal through your nervous system. Almost instantaneously you are sent into a state of fight or flight.

Have you ever thought there was a burglar in your home? You could've sworn you heard something. And before you knew it, your heart was beating quickly, your hands were sweaty, and your breath was shallow. Or have you ever thought you were going to get fired? You sat there, sure of it. You started worrying about what you're going to do now. You could see the conversation you'd have to have with your loved ones, explaining the situation to them. You could see the numbers in your bank account freeze. You want to hold on to that money because you don't know when more is coming. However, three months passed, and you were still working at the same job. You never got fired, but somehow you're still sure you will be.

The signals you send to your conscious mind create reactions throughout your central nervous system. When you understand how your mind works, you see that you can choose how things affect you—whether positively, negatively, or neutrally. When things upset you, protect yourself by asking: can I leave it at this and keep my peace and happiness?

Thoughts can let you down. Material things, situations, and people can let you down. One moment they were great, and then they made you feel lousy. He let me down. She let me down. It let me down. If you have expectations of people, places, or things they will, no matter how great they are, let you down at some point. Nothing is perfect, and our desire for our fantasies to become reality leaves us disappointed and living in an illusion. But we don't have to live this way; we can choose to stay happy.

For example, I just logged into my Twitter account, and there were a bunch of tweets from a reader of mine who said that I was "fake and pathetic" because she'd sent me an e-mail that I hadn't responded to yet. When I read this, my initial reaction was: How dare she? She doesn't even know me! But before that thought developed further, I reminded myself of this important success tool: don't take anything personally.

You never know what someone else is going through. Sometimes I forget this, and in this situation I almost felt like saying, "Only babies pout when they don't get what they want, because they know no other method." But that would be a reaction, taking her tweet personally. I had to remember that her comment probably had more to do with what was going on in her life than it did with me.

You never know what someone else is going through. If they can't give you what you want, it may be because their dad just died, or they have to deal with three hundred e-mails that day, or they have cancer, are traveling, or were just fired, or had a terribly traumatizing childhood or a bad week, or just got over the flu, or are dealing with some other constraint that their personal or work life has put on them. When someone seems to treat you unfairly, remember that they may be going through something crazy that they aren't telling you about.

There are many pitfalls to having expectations. People are going to do and say things you won't like, and you may never know why. But that's reality. So you have two choices. Think: How dare they? I can't believe it! This is ridiculous! Or think, this isn't worth losing my peace over. When things aren't going your way, ask yourself, is this worth losing my peace over? I'm sure that nine times out of ten it isn't.

Have you ever noticed that little things can upset you? Just tiny little things? Perhaps you are waiting in line and something is taking too long. Or perhaps someone didn't treat you with the respect you feel you deserve. Or how about while driving? Maybe the traffic light is taking too long to turn green and you feel personally insulted by it. You become frustrated and angry. Have you ever thought about how strange it is that people get so upset with others while driving? Many times people feel as though other drivers have made bad or unkind maneuvers just to insult them. Isn't that actually a hilarious concept? I mean, 99 percent of the time the drivers don't even know each other. How could either of them want to personally offend the other? Yet we can get angry at someone, as if they wanted to do it.

If a driver inches into your lane, you might react by saying, "How dare you?" But if a raindrop did the same thing, you would probably not get upset. You would probably not say to the raindrop, "How dare you?" Most of us (thankfully) don't take what a raindrop does personally. But we should all ask ourselves, do we get upset by these impersonal things that drift our way? If the answer is yes, it's not something to beat yourself up about. All you need to do is to start noticing it. That way you will become more aware of it. Check in with yourself: Uh-oh! What's going on? There's nothing to take personally. All is well. It was just the sky dropping rain on me. It was just a gust of wind blowing a leaf at me and nothing more.

At my last seminar, a young woman from Chicago began crying. She said her parents got divorced when she was four-teen and have been in a vicious routine ever since. Though they all live in the same small town just outside of Chicago, each wants to destroy the other and divide the children. She says both the parents speak of love and forgiveness but guilt their children when they go to the other side of town with the other parent. As she held back her tears in front of the other seminar attendees, she said her parents will even tell her they need to take a break from seeing her if she spends too much time with the other. When this happens the young woman said they stop speaking to her for weeks. She says it's so hard because each parent wants her to have no relationship with the other one. And they harbor resentment toward her if she does not conform to their unfair desires.

I let her keep talking in front of the seminar. According to her, the parents are enmeshed in legal battles and recently both became upset with her because they accused her of helping the other. This is why she was crying. "Every time my life is going great, they ruin it for me. I need to move from Chicago because they put me in the middle and use me!" she said.

"Do they use you? Or do they try to use you and you allow them to?" I asked.

"Well . . . why do they always have to do this to me? Why do they always have to say these things to me? I just don't get it, and it drives me nuts!" she said, in tears many of us can relate to.

I told her that it happens because it's happening. If you want to drive yourself mad, ask yourself why people do or say things you wish they wouldn't. You will never find an answer that brings you peace. Only *you* can bring yourself peace, and only *you* can take peace away from yourself. Instead of asking why this is happening to you, why they are doing this, ask yourself, how can I respond in a way that will allow me to keep my peace?

The surest path to angst, pain, and sadness is to expect people to do things they are incapable of doing. The young woman's parents are clearly incapable of being emotionally mature at this time in their lives. And they've shown this for the past ten or more years. Why expect them to be mature now? "Because it's the right thing to do," we think. So we hold them to a higher standard, an expectation equated with the norm. But what happens? They go off and act like little kids again and we feel the pain of it. Why do they have to do this again? we ask. They are supposed to be my parents! They are adults. Why do they do this to me? There is no sufficient answer so we slip into the role of victim. We tell ourselves, they are doing this thing to me and it's keeping me from my peace. But that is where we need to take a stand. The truth is, they are doing this thing and the way you are *reacting* is keeping you from your peace. The reality is that it's happening. No one knows why—you can rack your brain all you want in search of the answer, but it won't stop people from taking their course in life.

To find peace, grasp this simple truth: it is not what a person says or does that affects you but your reaction to what is said or done. I tell my friend these things and she begins to feel calm because she lets my words calm her. I then ask her to close her eyes and see and feel the world within her. Her world. Not her parents' world. What color is it? How does the life she desires feel? Those colors, those feelings, are her creation—not the creation of her parents nor anyone else.

What you see and how you feel are the product of *your* thinking and reactions. The world and the people you know will likely continue in their chaos. But you don't control that; it's outside you. And because it's outside you, it can't affect your thoughts unless you allow it to. No person or event can make you think anything you don't want to think. Why me? Why is this happening? That type of talk will negatively affect your world. Instead ask yourself how you can respond in a way that will keep your peace. That kind of self-talk will positively affect your world.

You can always choose to hold on to your peace even when responding to unfavorable situations. One way will cause you to feel like a victim at the mercy of people's actions and words, leaving you in pain and turmoil. The other will grant you the serenity to accept what happens with the wisdom to know what you can and can't change. It's always in your power to choose how you react.

People are all going on their own courses—some of their paths are favorable to yours and some aren't. It doesn't matter what they are doing or in which direction they go. What matters to you is your course, your direction. People can try to use you, upset you, stir emotions in you, and pull you out of your world. But that isn't what counts—what counts is if you let them.

If you are sitting in your car at a long stoplight and someone is playing music you can't stand (perhaps because it brings back bad memories), you don't have to listen to it and become upset. You can choose to roll up your window, turn on your own music, and go into your world with just a bit more volume. Or you can choose to keep your window down, hear their music, and say to yourself, "This too shall pass, and I will not let it ruin my day." Another choice is to say, "Why is this happening again? People are so dumb!" That may lead you back to thinking about the traumatizing experience that surrounds that song. However, feeling that way is your choice.

No one is making you think or do anything. Some people may wish they could and might even try to. They may pressure or guilt-trip you. But they can't make you think or do anything you would rather not.

Other people cannot annoy you, pain you, or irritate you *without your permission*. You have the creative power of thought. You can bless them and be on your way, or you can become emotionally controlled by them. If someone calls you something unpleasant, you have the freedom to say, "May peace fill your day." Remember this, and you will find peace where you once thought it impossible.

A beautiful, young, single mother inherited $75,000 when her grandfather died. Her parents told her the money was to be put into a retirement account so she would not touch it until she was older. That way she and her child would be secure.

One day, without any warning, her parents discovered that she had spent all the money on property near the desert. This made her parents angry. They vowed not to help take care of her or her child until she sold the land. In a fierce rage they went to the young mother with their demands. "Is that so?" was her only reply.

The woman continued to take great care of her investment. Five years passed and she had not communicated with her parents, though she had again and again reached out to them. One day a major land developer offered her three million dollars to develop her property into a mall. When the parents of the young lady heard this, they went to her, offered to take care of the child, and welcome them back into their lives. They asked for forgiveness and apologized profusely. The young lady happily handed them the child and invited them in for coffee. As they apologized and tried to explain themselves, the young lady simply responded, "Is that so?"

People are often irrational, cruel, and lacking in empathy. You must continue onward anyway. The noise of the world doesn't need to play louder than the music you're dancing to. When someone says something you'd rather not have heard, they aren't making you think it. When sound goes into your ears in the form of undesirable news, it is not a record player that must repeat in your head. The feelings of stress or fear that others project onto you are just that—projections. When you sit in front of a white wall and watch a movie projected on it, you know it's not real. It's just a movie. The images from the film are not staining your white wall. They are playing until they are done, and then they are over. The white wall that was once covered with projected images is clear again.

The human mind is that white wall. People are projectors. They want to relieve themselves of their fear or angst, so they project it onto those around them. We can choose to be like the white wall, asking, "Is that so? Isn't that interesting?" We can watch the sounds and images fade away. Or we can believe that what is being projected onto us is absolute. We can cause ourselves more stress than we can handle by choosing to take what happens or what someone says personally. It's not personal—it's just happening. When we take things personally we allow people and circumstances to affect us, but this is our choice—they don't have to.

For many of us, our mantra is, "I can't believe this is happening to me." But to maintain the highest, best, and most peaceful version of ourselves, we should instead say, "Is this so? Isn't that interesting?" Things are not happening to you; they are happening around you. You can react to them if you wish, but soon they will change.

I was extremely excited when a major public-speaking agency decided to represent me. I flew across the country to meet the team and get my speech topics in place so they could begin booking me. The opportunity meant big money, a lot of travel, a lot of events, and a lot of fun. I could see the future, and it was magnificent.

After the meeting I was so pleased at how well it went. Everyone had big smiles and anticipated big things. I flew home feeling very grateful. That night I was so happy to see my booking page on their website, next to some of my favorite professional speakers.

However, the next morning I received an e-mail informing me that I was not a good fit for the company, and they went ahead and deleted me from the website. I was devastated: Why would they have me fly out? Don't they get it? I can't believe I just spent all that time and money going all the way there!

For the rest of the day, I was very upset. I took what they said personally. I felt completely rejected. My hopes were soaring in the air and suddenly the wind stopped. I felt stranded in a stormy ocean with no sight of shore. I was so shocked and embarrassed that I pretended as if nothing had happened. I denied it to myself. When people asked, I pretended all was well with the agency—when in reality they had dropped me. I didn't want to believe it, because it interfered with what I wanted to hear.

Eventually, I tried to make sense of it all: Maybe I'm just not good enough. Maybe this career isn't going to work out. I'll probably never get opportunities because of this.

It wasn't until a few days had passed that I took a closer look. Most unpleasant experiences are due to our inability to accept reality. We fight and argue with reality, even though that can't change anything. Someone had said something that I didn't want to hear, and I took it as a personal insult and allowed it to temporarily ruin my life. And as it turned out, a better opportunity came up after my disappointment.

We have to trust that life is moving the way it should. We can't take life's events personally. We need to find a way to be resilient and move forward with joy, no matter the circumstances.

On my last speaking tour, a seventeen-year-old high school senior was in tears after my speech. She explained that she had been accepted into the college of her dreams but that she was not allowed to go. Her father told her that she had to stay home, get a job, pay their rent, and make money to take care of her seven siblings. She was devastated. She thought it was the worst thing that could possibly happen to her. I asked her why she had to take care of her family.

"When I was little," she began, "I used to think everyone's mom made a living by selling themselves, by trafficking to make money. Most people's childhood memories consist of family vacations, fights between siblings, and beach days. Mine are more along the lines of fighting with clients, living in motel rooms, and seeing angry drunks who wanted more—they always wanted more. It was normal to me, and looking back now, it was normal in all the wrong ways. I have recently made a decision, a promise to myself—I not only refuse to succumb to the lifestyle that I was raised with, but I am empathetic and determined to help others avoid living this way.

"I've blurred out almost all the memories I have with my mom, there are only a handful that seem real—they are so vivid that they replay themselves over and over again in my head. My mom was only thirteen years old when she started trafficking and doing drugs—thirteen years old when she made the decision that has impacted an entire family and made me the person I am today. Back when I was young, San Diego was beaming with new trafficking opportunities. Up until I was ten years old, we made the train trip to all the same spots, all our old haunts. I found comfort in the hotels we stayed at, even the shabbiest Motel 6, because they always guaranteed my mom and baby brother would have a place to stay. This does not mean that our situation didn't trouble me. One day I came to her devastated because my eight-year-old brain had convinced itself that I was the reason she was homeless. She used to pay me out of her weekly earnings. Whether it was an act of bribery to keep me quiet, or a simple notion of her guilt, I was paid one hundred dollars almost every weekend we were together. I was convinced that I was like any other spoiled little girl—that I was the reason she sold her body. It wasn't until years later that I realized something felt wrong, and that I felt dirty keeping her secret.

"Coping with it became harder as I grew older. On the days she couldn't find any buyers, we would sit outside our local gas stations and Walmart, holding a simple sign: 'Children hungry. God Bless.' I found myself questioning any values I had: Why would anyone want to bless a family like mine? We didn't deserve it. Watching someone I loved live like that was hard. But this life was all we had.

"I have not fully wrapped my head around the way my mom left, and I have so many questions that I will never get to ask her. However, the things she taught me in the time I did have with her are lessons far greater and more important than anything I could have learned in a textbook. And she taught me all this without realizing it. She taught me that kindness and one's ability to think for themselves are what matters. She taught me strength through her weakness and love through her sacrifice. She taught me to see beauty in the world. I am beyond thankful for what I have and I do not let a day go by without reminding myself of what truly matters. I want to take the beautiful, unique, eccentric life I have been given to travel and teach children who are less fortunate.

"I am now seventeen years old. I live with my father, who constantly struggles with alcohol abuse, and a few of my brothers and sisters. I am a graduating senior and I am proud to say that I was accepted to the University of Hawaii at Manoa, my dream school. Unfortunately, due to financial reasons at home, I am staying here in California and working to help my family.

"I am a witness of the heartache trafficking and drug abuse can cause, not a victim. I am empathetic and determined to help. I want to take the experience I was given and turn it into something that can help people in similar situations. I want to make a difference in the lives of real people—in a real and impactful way. If just a few unsavory individuals can cause so much havoc, then a single person like me, motivated to make an impact, can go on to produce the previously unimaginable. I can, and I know that I will. I know that my family was not the only one that set up shop at the local Motel 6."

Does that story not shake you to your core? The wind blew in a way this young woman would've preferred it not to. She could've blamed herself or let it be the reason her life would fall apart. I wouldn't have blamed her for choosing to do so. Hers sounds like one of the best and most legitimate reasons to be depressed and angry that I've ever heard. But she chose to do the opposite. She adjusted her sail, found the value in her experience, and is determined to use it for good.

It's easy to get mad at the world and take a cynical view—it requires less effort than figuring out how to move forward. But like the classical Greek tragedian Euripides said, "And why should we feel anger at the world? As if the world would notice." Summed up a little differently, Jim Rohn once said, "Wishing for a different wind is naïve at best."

In life, things happen that we don't want, and we are often dealt cards we don't want. Sometimes we give up peace, for all our life, trying to understand why something happened to us. And because we never find the right answers, we never get our peace back. But what the world needs is more people who flow like water—more people who go around the rock that obstructs the course of their stream. Not those who stop and say, "What the heck, rock! Why did you block my flow?" Instead, we adjust accordingly and stay with the flow. We must continually ask ourselves what we can learn from this situation or person. Is it worth losing your peace over what happened? You can always learn, and you can always keep your peace.

EXERCISE FOR

CREED FIVE

- When someone tells you something undesirable, practice the mantra, "Is that so? Isn't that interesting?" Put yourself into a space where you do not react and take personal offense. Ask yourself, "Is this worth losing my peace over?" Write it on a sticky note and stick it on the side of your computer screen.

CREED SIX

Stay Open and Vulnerable

WHEN YOU WERE a little kid, you probably experienced times when you couldn't sleep because you were terrified of monsters under your bed. Your hands may have gotten clammy while your nervous system pumped adrenaline into your body, paralyzing you with fear. You probably screamed for your mom and dad, hoping that someone would come into your room so you could stop feeling like an anxious wreck.

Then when your mom looked under the bed, you realized there was no monster there—the monster wasn't real; it just *felt* real. In fact, while it was happening, it felt *extremely* real—this is because your nervous system was reacting to it as though it were real. Stress hormones were pumped into your body to deal with the thoughts you created about the monster under your bed: "There's a monster under my bed! I need to protect myself. I need to run from this thing." Your nervous system tried to protect you from the monster because although the harm wasn't real, the perception in your mind was.

We are intelligent creatures and, as such, we naturally want to protect ourselves—our survival depends on it. Therefore our nervous systems release hormones so we can choose "fight or flight" to protect ourselves. This fosters the evolution of our species.

However, today we don't often need to protect ourselves from a tiger or a bear, which is why we developed this fight-or-flight response in the first place. And yet we still can't sleep because we think there are monsters under our bed. Even as adults, the metaphoric monsters under our bed make our eyes bulge and our palms sweaty as we try to sleep at night. We become full of anxiety and fear because we are afraid to experience new relationships, to reach new financial goals, to become better leaders, to ask someone out, or to connect with our coworkers by diving past the superficiality of casual conversation.

Dive into something real! Expose your true self. Be authentic. Be yourself. Put yourself out on a limb. Don't let the monsters under your bed convince you that you will fail, be rejected, feel pain, get hurt, lose, feel dumb, or be gobbled up if you open yourself up.

When we ask ourselves, "What's the worst that could happen if I try?" our minds begin to focus on the worst possible scenarios. We envision ourselves failing, and we want to avoid feeling the bitterness or pain we may experience if things don't work out. The *story we create* about our fear pumps us with adrenaline, which causes a real experience of fear and stops us from being who we want to be. We remain static as a way to protect ourselves. We opt out of opening our hearts to those around us and reaching our true potential. We stop choosing to do the little things that make the world a better place—like smiling at strangers—for fear that we will be rejected or hurt.

People say that courage isn't the absence of fear but rather the choice to continue to do something even when you are afraid. Courage is taking a deep breath and looking under your bed. Facing our fears is much easier than living with the terror created by focusing on fear—those nights that we lie in bed, losing sleep because we are scared that the monsters will get us; the times when we are stressed, anxious, unhappy, and missing out on living to our full potential. Look under the bed: you may find that the monsters don't exist.

Many people are so afraid of living that they numb themselves constantly—they become addicted to alcohol, drugs, food, television, the Internet, or busyness—bypassing *real* human experiences. We are all scared of pain, rejection, failing—of being vulnerable. But we can't tell ourselves that our fears are more important than our dreams. We can't stop believing in living with true happiness. Don't let the negative stories in your head stop you from living the way you want to. Remember, courage isn't the absence of fear. It is the act of embracing fear. It is doing the things that scare you.

To live is to be open to the world. Send out your love, look people in the eyes, smile a bigger smile than you ever have. Do things you never thought you could and play on a wider field than you ever imagined. Ask yourself if your deepest fears, stories, and excuses are only silly monsters under your bed.

Start to look under the bed more often, in more areas of life, in all experiences and dreams. Only then can you find out how powerful, beautiful, and loving you can become. Only then can you find out how great you really are.

Are monsters preventing you from making more money and gaining financial freedom? What monsters are stopping you from having more joy and better health? Which ones are stopping you from living new experiences? Often we don't know where to begin when we want to become more valuable to the marketplace, to the world, and to ourselves, but asking ourselves these questions can really help. They're vital.

So what monsters are under your bed?

Unfortunately, most people aren't willing to get messy. That's what I've noticed in meeting tens of thousands of people this year, while speaking at a high school, college, or organization almost every day. You don't need better teeth, a finer set of breasts, bigger biceps, washboard abs, a better education, or the right car to get the lover you wish for or to make your dreams come true. And you don't need to fix your past or wait until you have everything figured out. The barrier to living your dream life is not how you look, where you've been, what you've done, or how well you've prepared. The barrier is that there are not enough scars on your heart and there are far too few failures to your name. The trouble is that your hands are not dirty enough and your heart isn't beating fast enough from nervousness at having to face your fears.

For too long we've believed that we must arrive at the finish line looking clean, pretty, and perfect. And we've believed that if we aren't ready now, we should wait until we are good enough. But the time to believe this is over. The truth is that to reach any goal you must feel the wind crack your lips and the warm, moist sweat dribble off your hands. Your body must perspire from anxiety because you feel you cannot possibly face your fears—and yet you are facing them, which is scaring you half to death.

To reach any goal, you must feel your nerves and allow yourself to look like a mess from repetitive failure. If this happens, you will be much closer to reaching your goal. Remember, even a star collapses on itself before it bursts forth into the galaxy. Get going for what you think you aren't good enough to go after—for what truly makes you vibrate with fear and excitement inside. Then, once you begin to go for it, you will be blown in every direction, but it will feel amazing because you will be taking steps toward something you believe in. And when the voice in your head says you look like a fool, or when you fall, or when you feel unqualified in appearance or intelligence, tell that voice that *your beauty is your vulnerability*. Be brave, fall hard, and get going against the wind.

It's scary putting yourself out there, regardless of what you're doing. Whether you are asking someone out, sharing intimate feelings, asking for a raise, giving a compliment, sharing an idea you are passionate about, starting a new business, giving a speech, starting to play an instrument or picking it back up again, working on a creative project, standing up for what you believe, or most anything else, there is a possibility that it won't go well. And it's dangerous to dance in that uncertainty, in that place of the unknown. There are no guarantees that you won't feel damaged or pained as a result of stepping out on a limb for something you want or believe in.

As an aspiring author, my dream-life bubble started to deflate when every publisher I approached told me my first book was not sellable. I heard it all: There's no market for this. You're too young. The book needs work. Become famous and then write books after. Build an online readership. But the most unsettling and scary thing I heard was, "Self-publish this book and sell ten thousand copies—then you can get a publisher. Start by making your Facebook fan page and putting yourself out there." Putting myself out there? Out there, into the world where I might be rejected, judged, and belittled? I wanted to say no thanks and simply collect my check from a major publisher, travel the world on book tours, inspire people, and have a lot of fun. But step number one was to make a Facebook fan page. I figured it was easy enough, so I made it.

I can still remember starting the page. "Jake Ducey has 1 Like," I read on the computer screen. And that one Like was from me, from my personal Facebook account. So it really should've said, "Jake Ducey likes himself." I was terrified and felt like a failure, though I had just barely begun. My mom hadn't even liked the page yet! I had invited my friends to the page, but none of them had liked it yet either. No luck.

I scrolled down the Facebook newsfeed. I read the status

update of a guy I'd gone to high school with. It said, "Jake Ducey invites you to like his new fan page. YEAH RIGHT! HAHA." I was devastated. I'd put myself out there and been totally rejected. Humiliated! I felt so embarrassed.

I started asking myself if I was good enough, smart enough. I felt like the whole world thought I was an idiot. I assumed no one would ever care about my message. And then, lo and behold, the sting wore off. After a few days, with time, everything grew. I ended up selling those ten thousand copies of the book and many more. Publishers were impressed and started taking me seriously.

Two years later, while riding a total high from the momentum I'd gathered after allowing myself to be vulnerable, I pulled up to a 7-Eleven in San Diego, where I'd gone to high school. I hopped out of the car to fill up my gas tank, and standing in the middle of the gas station roundabout, with a Big Gulp in his hand, was the guy who had written the humiliating and rejecting Facebook status update about me and my dream. I saw him, and my body instantly tensed up. It was as if my brain, muscles, and nervous system remembered the pain that he symbolized for me. The last time I'd had an interaction with him, it had just about killed my self-esteem. My body instinctually tried to protect itself and turned away.

As I turned I heard, "Jake Ducey!" He was yelling my name. I walked to him with a fake smile, scared out of my mind. To my amazement, as it was noon on a random day in the middle of the week, he was drunk out of his mind. He was so intoxicated that he hardly made sense. "So you're like a big-time author now or something, huh?" he said. "Not big time, but I'm working on a new book now," I responded. He just looked at me. I could feel him studying me. He looked me up and down, and I smiled in defense. "Well, it was good to see you. I hope you're doing well!" I said, while I shuffled away. He said nothing and looked at me, while I hopped into my car and drove away.

If it hasn't happened already, you'll be amazed by the kinds of belittling things people will say about you. It can feel demoralizing. It feels safer to stay small, guarded, and protected within yourself. We often tell ourselves not to reach too far or stretch too much—it could all be taken away. But author Elizabeth Appell explains that it's more painful to hide who we are than to put ourselves out there: "And the day came when the risk to remain tight in a bud was more painful than the risk it took to blossom."

We spend too much time attempting to outwit vulnerability by keeping ourselves within comfortable—but small and protected—ways of living. Our inability to face fear and find freedom in the discomfort of terrifying acts—like speaking our mind, trying something new, becoming a leader, taking the time to hear people out, giving compliments we're normally too busy to give, or sharing our ideas—leads to our not doing these things, because we believe it's safer to remain tight in a bud. But the truth is that staying closed creates more pain than the potential rejection and anxiety you will face when trying to get open and blossom.

Actor Ashton Kutcher says: "Vulnerability is the essence of romance. It's the art of being uncalculated, the willingness to look foolish, the courage to say, 'This is me, and I'm interested in you enough to show you my flaws with the hope that you may embrace me for all that I am but, more important, all that I am not.'"

Vulnerability is the essence of economic and career success, as well as personal fulfillment. No matter what you do, where you are, or what you're after, at a certain point you have to summon the courage to say: This is what I believe. This is me, and I'm willing to show my flaws, speak my mind, and face my fears with the hope that it will make me more valuable to the world and more free within myself.

Imagine that I ask you to be a leader at work, even to lead people who are higher up and more respected at the company. And that I want you to do this by connecting with people in a way that stimulates and inspires them, that makes them feel appreciated and motivated. I need you to stop looking down when you get up from your desk. I need you to smile at people when you walk down the hall or take your break. I need you to ask them how they are doing—to listen to them, encourage them, and compliment them. I need you to lovingly acknowledge people you do not ordinarily pay attention to. And I need you to adapt to this change immediately and fluidly.

Or imagine that I ask you to come up with a new idea at work—a creative and innovative idea. I need you to come up with a solution to a problem or write out a proposal for a new way of doing things at the company. You're going to share it with everyone in the company, even with your bosses. Some people will not take the time to read it. Some people will think it's stupid. And some people will think it's a bad idea. Others won't even understand it. But I assure you that some people will like it and be inspired by it. We need creativity and innovation, and we're counting on you to spark it in everyone else right now.

If I asked you to do either of these things, your palms might get sweaty. You might develop shortness of breath. You might start thinking about what could go wrong if you did this or that. Your body might get warmer and less comfortable. Your nervous system might start pumping stress hormones to signal that it needs to protect itself. You might feel vulnerable, and you might try to close yourself down.

When we have an opportunity in work or love, we think we have to be perfect—we think we aren't yet good enough. Our culture thinks of vulnerability as a weak and dark emotion. We think: I am afraid. I am uncertain. Therefore

I am at risk. This is bad. I must protect myself and shut myself down so I'm not exposed too much. I am shy. I don't want to feel this. I don't want to be uncomfortable. I will not let myself be vulnerable.

Vulnerability expert Dr. Brené Brown says that vulnerability feels like the birthplace of everything bad, but it's also the birthplace of freedom, joy, and connection. The remedy for feeling vulnerable is courage. In our culture we think courage is perfection—being fearless, brave, and strong, clobbering anything that comes our way, being invincible. In fact, it's the opposite. This is how Nelson Mandela defined it: "Courage is not the absence of fear, but the triumph over it. The brave man is not he who does not feel afraid, but he who conquers that fear."

Courage is the ability to feel like you may not be good enough to increase your income, become a leader through example, learn a new skill, or make a person smile and feel loved, but you make the attempt, and in the act you uncover a new sense of freedom and joy. You feel more connected to those around you. You step outside your box and find dormant forces and energies within you that open up a whole new way of living and working in the world.

Some of us wonder, can I give my whole self to this? But instead of asking what's the worst that can happen, we have to start wondering, *if I finally do this, what's the best that can happen?* What's the best that can happen if I finally take that next step in my life? What's the best that can happen if I authentically try to connect with the people whose paths I cross on a daily basis? What's the best that can happen if I ask that person out on a date? What's the best that can happen if I smile and start a conversation with someone I would ordinarily just walk past?

I'll admit, saying hi first, getting fired, working hard for a raise, asking someone out on a date, giving someone you don't know a compliment, and trying something new are all scary things to do. What if I fail? What if they don't understand me? What if they think I'm stupid, ugly, or not good enough? What will happen if I do this? There's no guarantee it will work out. What if I put my all into this and it flops? Yes, these things are all a bit scary because they make us vulnerable—they crack our shell. But that's what this world is for—it's a place where to be free you must expose yourself. Otherwise we are just hiding behind masks and default behaviors that work only to protect us from imagined rejection and untested feelings of unworthiness.

We must remember that being vulnerable also means being deeply grounded in our five senses. When we live and work from a place that says, "I may feel afraid, but I'm going to open myself up despite this anxiety," we begin to inspire everyone around us to slowly come out of their shell too. We begin to see how strong and worthy we really are. We begin to trust ourselves more. And we begin to feel more connected to those around us and to the work we do, even where we once felt disengaged.

This is the best way to increase our value, and thus our earnings in the world. Whether you clean floors, work in an office, teach students, are an artist, entrepreneur, or run a major company, you can become a leader by stepping out of your shell. That courageous energy is contagious. People notice it consciously and feel it unconsciously.

When you connect with those around you, people notice it and begin to reciprocate. You can inspire people and shift the culture of your work or home. When you take the step, your gesture invites others to do the same. People begin to open themselves up, to be seen and heard, which allows them to see and hear others as well.

Being vulnerable may seem like a weakness, but perhaps it's our biggest strength. It helps us become the greatest version of ourselves. It allows us to have more courage, connection, love, passion, and creativity.

The great writer C. S. Lewis once said: "To love at all is to be vulnerable. Love anything and your heart will be wrung and possibly broken. If you want to make sure of keeping it intact, you must give it to no one, not even an animal. Wrap it carefully round with hobbies and little luxuries; avoid all entanglements. Lock it up safe in the casket or coffin of your selfishness. But in that casket, safe, dark, motionless, airless, it will change. It will not be broken; it will become unbreakable, impenetrable, irredeemable. To love is to be vulnerable."

This truth is not limited to romantic love. If you live fully, you can put your heart into anything, regardless of whether it's a person, place, project, or idea. You cannot give your all to the projects I proposed to you earlier in this chapter if you are not vulnerable. If I ask you to turn something in at work or step outside what you normally do, you run the risk of rejection or of being misunderstood. Naturally you will want to protect yourself—you will not want to show up fully. This is what Lewis is talking about in the quote above. It's protecting yourself from getting hurt, from being vulnerable, and thus choosing to live a life without love or passion.

Inadequacy is a common fear among people who want to be leaders or to achieve something great in their lives. We may be bigger and better than we've ever been, but that doesn't mean the larger public will immediately recognize it. It's that feeling of putting our all into something and not getting what we expect back. It's reaching out to someone with compassion and then getting shut down or going unnoticed. These feelings are not fun, but they are feelings that leaders must feel.

Winners do not know if they are equipped for the task, but they take the necessary steps to find out. They aren't sure if they can make more money or fall in love, but they give their heart to it fully anyway. And they usually end up finding out that they are more capable than they had thought. Their newfound confidence and the empathy that grows from vulnerability become an inspiration to those around them. Maybe they are happier and more fulfilled than ever before. You can feel joy emanate from them. They are no longer shy or afraid to speak up and listen closely. They have broken out of their shell, shared their ideas, and trusted their creative intuition.

When you find the courage to grow, you are more valued at work and more connected and joyful at home. Vulnerability can paralyze us, but it can also make us stronger. We can no longer allow fear, self-doubt, shyness, nervousness, rejection, and stress to stop us from living our lives fully. We have to open up. We can't keep closing ourselves off and missing opportunities. We need to embrace the fear and stop trying to play it safe. If we continue to live this way, we will continue to feel disconnected. We will continue to numb ourselves.

Statistically speaking, America's population is frighteningly unfulfilled, medicated, obese, and depressed. This is not only a reflection of what's happening in our personal lives but also of how we feel at work. It comes from our lack of courage to be vulnerable.

It's ironic that we've convinced ourselves that in the workplace we need to do the opposite of heart-centered things like opening up and compassionately connecting with others.

Writer John Steinbeck eloquently says, "It always seemed strange to me that the things we admire in men: kindness and generosity, openness, honesty, understanding, and feeling are the concomitants of failure in our system. And those traits we detest: sharpness, greed, acquisitiveness, meanness, egotism, and self-interest are the traits of success."

Deep within us, we know that it is admirable and important to be open and selfless, but our culture has built its success on egotism and shutting oneself off from others. This lack of vulnerability, of authenticity, of realness and openness in our hearts and emotions, is ruining happiness—not only at work, but also in society at large.

What we need to consider is that fear of being open and vulnerable can paralyze us, and yet facing that fear can make us stronger. We have to break the barrier and open ourselves up to the people and things around us. We may fail, but if we don't try, we imprison ourselves. Opening yourself and your heart, even in a world full of constant letdowns and no guarantees, is the way to becoming your best self. You need to have the courage to be vulnerable.

Sometimes we lock ourselves into situations so tightly that we can hardly even breathe. Sometimes we run imaginary scenarios through our heads about the worst things that can happen if we make certain decisions: This may happen, therefore I cannot do that. There's no guarantee it will go well, and I don't want to be rejected, so I'm not going to do it—it's for my own good. Sound familiar?

Sometimes the thoughts in our heads about what may or may not happen if we do x, y, or z are even more debilitating than the actual experiences. This is because there's no action or remedy to take that will change them. Our breath gets shorter and our hands get sweatier. If that's the case, if your mind is blocking you from being vulnerable and being seen, you need to start by being aware that it's happening: uh-oh, I'm worrying and feeling fearful again because my mind and body can't tell the difference between an actual event outside and what's going on inside my head.

Your nervous system thinks you're being threatened and produces stress hormones to signal danger and call for protection. Then you shut down your heart and courage. There may be times when the thoughts racing in your mind have such a strong gravitational pull that you can't get yourself out of them right away. But with practice, the time it takes for you to realize that it's just your mind—that it's not reality—will shorten. You will begin to spot these thoughts, fears, and worries and to separate yourself from them.

If you don't take time to develop awareness about these kinds of thoughts, your nervous system will produce more stress hormones and try to protect you. It will close you off from your immediate environment. The body reacts whether a threat is legitimate or not. It produces the same energy whether a burglar is really in the house or not. It responds to what the mind tells it is true. When this happens, you simply need to be aware that it's just your thoughts and fears, and to remember that you can triumph over them with courage. You can even take a conscious, deep breath and step out of your racing mind. Otherwise you will start to believe that the only way to protect yourself is to shut down. When you allow this to happen, your heart shuts down. On a neurobiological level, you stop fulfilling your need for connection with the people and world around you. Eventually, however, when you step outside these fearful thoughts and become present once again, it's like waking up from a nightmare. Your thoughts may try to pull you back in, but the more you become aware of them, the more you can protect yourself. That's why it's so important to have an awareness practice like meditation, yoga, walking, journaling, or some other activity that pulls you back into the present. The more you practice, the less you will find yourself trapped by these negative and fearful thoughts.

Although feelings of vulnerability may seem a prison, they're actually your greatest stepping-stones to freedom. They empower you to be courageous and to overcome your feelings of unworthiness and fear. When we realize that courage is not the absence of fear or doubt but the ability to do things regardless of fear or doubt, we generate confident, connected, and passionate energy. We stop yielding to resistance, separation, and fear.

You feel a greater sense of belonging and fulfillment when you start connecting with those around you. Your confidence grows. You start to see how much you have to offer to the world. You see how your seemingly small choices can actually make a big difference. You become more valuable at work, and your presence empowers others to step outside their own shells. At home you are more respected, acknowledged, and understood.

Author Stephen Russell says: "Vulnerability is the only authentic state. Being vulnerable means being open, for wounding, but also for pleasure. Being open to the wounds of life means also being open to the bounty and beauty. Don't mask or deny your vulnerability: it is your greatest asset. Be vulnerable: quake and shake in your boots with it. The new goodness that is coming to you, in the form of people, situations, and things, can only come to you when you are vulnerable, i.e. open."

In 1990, when NASA's Voyager 1 space probe took the famous photograph *Pale Blue Dot*, it was at a record distance of 3.7 billion miles from Earth. The photo was taken from so far away that each pixel took five and a half hours, traveling at the speed of light, to reach Earth. In the picture, our planet is shown as a fraction of a pixel (0.12 pixels in size), floating in infinite space.

American astronomer Carl Sagan once said, "Earth is a very small stage in a vast cosmic arena." It's a speck of dust, and in our delusion we believe it has great importance. We clench our jaws and rack our minds, worrying about how our life's events will play out. Think of the rivers of sweat created by all those folks perspiring anxiously, worrying their way into their graves. All so they can, for a blink in eternity, stand at the top of this minuscule, fractionated pixel called Earth. We are a micropixel atop a demipixel, floating through endless space—space that our minds can't even comprehend because it is so vast. That alone should encourage us to buckle our seat belts and enjoy this space ride. Unfortunately, it most often doesn't.

Instead, we choose to neglect one another. We judge others. We make them wrong. We blame them. We claw and scratch our way to success and a sense of significance while thinking, "Do you remember that guy who quit? Me neither. Work hard and be remembered." Yet most scientists accept the likelihood that the human race will become extinct in five billion years. None of our earthly artifacts will survive. All our statues and memorials to achievers will disappear into nothing. The sun will have sizzled our planet into a molten crisp. And yet we continue to destroy ourselves.

What are we striving for? Why do we need to be fearful and submissive, slaving away at a computer in hopes to be remembered? Inevitably, we will be forgotten—we will all dissolve back into dust. Why do we need to shut ourselves down and keep ourselves from discovering the best and most powerful version of who we are? Why do we need to wait for a raise when we can work on becoming valuable now—and by default earn that raise? Why do we need to feel alone when there are so many beautiful people around us who we can create a connection with? Why do we need to wait to become an executive or have a bunch of awards to be a great leader? Why do we do all this when we can choose to be a powerful inspiration and a valuable person now?

Steve Jobs got it wrong. We will not dent the universe. Thinking that's possible is like an ant wishing to make its mark on the Empire State Building—impossible. But what we can do is make a dent in another person's life. The purpose of our lives on this tiny pixel is to be courageous, to love, and to become a light in the infinite darkness of space. We can strive to die knowing that we stayed open, vulnerable, and that we loved. You will likely not be remembered in a thousand years, but you can shine your light. Light is who you are—light that only your misunderstanding dims.

The key to success is as simple as keeping watch over your inner light, making sure that you are shining brightly and staying open and available for those who need you. When we commit to living with awareness and connecting with others, we can have anything we want because we become more valuable.

Don't stay too locked into the illusions of this world and lose sight of what's important. Make different choices. Live by these six creeds. You can find purpose and fulfillment in life. You can choose to remember what's most important. Live your life as a shining light that makes a difference.

EXERCISE FOR

CREED SIX

■ What barriers have you put up to keep the pain out? What masks do you wear so you won't look foolish? Drop them. Step out of your shell and allow yourself to be a beautiful mess. When you feel too nervous to compliment someone and you're tempted not to, go and compliment them. When you're tempted to stay quiet, instead let someone know you appreciate them. Do those things that make your heart beat quicker. Let down your walls, as they are keeping the love out too.

Dear fellow human being,

I know your time is very valuable and that you have many things you could be doing. So thank you for picking up this book. Now that it is over, let the real practice begin.

My intention is *not* that these lessons will be read by millions of people and translated into many languages. That was certainly my goal for my first few books. However, I must admit, it was a shallow goal.

Now I would like to close this book the same way I close my weekend seminars, the "True You" Retreat.

My intention and prayer is that these messages will be genuinely practiced. The real learning begins when this book is put down and the busyness of your life strikes again. The journey begins when you head off to your busy week and you get overwhelmed. It starts with the people right around you. Have you resorted to your old ways of ducking your head and avoiding connection and smiling, or are you stepping outside yourself and your personal concerns to brighten someone else's moment?

The world has plenty of ambitious people. It has plenty of hard workers. What we need more of are loving and generous people who despite the intoxicating temptation to duck their heads, close their hearts, get back to work, and use the excuse of "busyness" do not neglect their biggest calling: lift the fallen, restore the broken, and heal the hurting.

This is a great undertaking and begins in our homes, while we're at the store, and while we're walking through the hallways at work.

The question I hope you continue to ask yourself is, how can I bring joy, inspiration, and relief to those around me?

Please, do not be too shy to step outside yourself.

I hope you'll reach out to me on Facebook, Twitter, YouTube, or Instagram: @JakeDucey.

I also hope to see you at one of my "True You" Retreats.

Send me a line: Jake@JakeDucey.com.

Thank you,
Jake Ducey